T0045813

# the
# **Christian**
# Leader

# Other Books by Bill Hull

*Jesus Christ, Disciplemaker*
*The Disciple - Making Pastor*
*The Disciple - Making Church*
*Straight Talk on Spiritual Power*
*Christlike*
*The Complete Book of Discipleship*
*Choose the Life*
*Anxious for Nothing*
*Right Thinking*
*Building High Commitment in a Low Commitment World*
*Seven Steps to Transform Your Church*

**The Experience the Life Series (with Paul Mascarella)**
*Believe as Jesus Believed*
*Live as Jesus Lived*
*Love as Jesus Loved*
*Minister as Jesus Ministered*
*Lead as Jesus Led*

*Conversion and Discipleship* (2016)
*Evangelism and Discipleship*
(with Bobby Harrington, 2014)
*The False Promise of Discipleship*
(with Brandon Cook, 2016)

# the
# **Christian**
# Leader

Rehabilitating Our Addiction
to Secular Leadership

## Bill Hull

ZONDERVAN

*The Christian Leader*
Copyright © 2016 by Robert W. Hull

This title is also available as a Zondervan ebook. Visit www.zondervan.com/ebooks.

Requests for information should be addressed to:
Zondervan, 3900 Sparks Dr. SE, Grand Rapids, Michigan 49546

Library of Congress Cataloging-in-Publication Data

Hull, Bill, 1946-
    The Christian leader : rehabilitating our addiction to secular leadership /
    Bill Hull.
        pages cm
    Includes bibliographical references.
    ISBN 978-0-310-52533-2 (softcover)
    1. Leadership – Religious aspects – Christianity. I. Title.
BV4597.53.L43H84   2016
253 – dc23                                                        2015035321

Cover design: LUCAS Art and Design
Interior design: Kait Lamphere

Printed in the United States of America

16 17 18 19 20 21 22 23 24 25 26 /DHV/ 15 14 13 12 11 10 9 8 7 6 5 4 3 2 1

*To Coach Gene Ring, my first leader*

# Contents

# Foreword

**MY LIFE CHANGED** forever on November 22, 1999 when an 18-wheeler rear-ended me at sixty-five miles per hour on a high-rise bridge in New Orleans, Louisiana. My Ford Mustang plowed into the guard rail, dislodging my seat from the hinges as my seatbelt locked. My body torqued, injuring two discs in my back and two in my neck.

After getting X-rays, the doctor said to me, "Mr. Gallaty, it's a miracle that you're not hurt worse than you are." He then sent me home with four prescriptions: Oxycontin, Valium, Soma, and Percocet. I was twenty-two years old, and I had never taken drugs before. But because of the pain from the accident, I started taking them every four to six hours. In three months, I was addicted to pharmaceutical drugs.

I soon realized that my thirty-day supply was only going to last two weeks and I was desperate for another avenue to stay high. Two friends approached me with a way to fuel my drug addiction, and building on my background in the business world I started an illegal-drug import business. I was trafficking in the city — GHB, Special-K, heroin, cocaine, marijuana — and by the world's standards, life was good ... at least for a season.

That next year, a close friend unexpectedly died of a heroin overdose, which kicked off a troubling series of events. Over the next three years, from 2000 to 2003, I lost eight friends to drug- and alcohol-related deaths. Six others went to jail. Through all of this, my addiction was slowly destroying my life. I was spending around $180 a day to fuel my desire for heroin and cocaine.

After two unsuccessful stints in rehab, I recalled the words a college friend had shared with me one night seven years earlier. He had spoken to me about Christ and the hope of the gospel, and as I looked at the mess of my life, I knew I had a problem. I cried out for help. I wasn't in a church or a revival service. I was just sitting in my room, but I called out for Jesus to rescue me. The date was November 12, 2002.

Like anyone who has been saved from heinous and deep-rooted patterns of sin, the transformation in my life was remarkable. My life has not been the same since that moment. I immediately realized that the reason why I had failed twice at rehab was because I'd been trying to get freedom from my addictions *apart* from the liberating power of Jesus. I now knew that Jesus was the only one who could remove the chains of sin that had kept me shackled and bound for so many years.

Today, over a decade later, I'm a Christian leader — a pastor. I've come to understand that the first step of *any* rehabilitation is an awareness of the problem. Not all Christian leaders will walk the road of addiction that I followed, but we all have blind spots in our lives and ministries. And they are called blind spots for a reason — if we could see them, we'd fix them! Like a cancer growing undetected in our bodies, every leader has specific pitfalls that will eventually sabotage them if they aren't addressed.

I never wanted to be an addict. I've never met a pastor or leader who wanted to be a narcissist or a dictator or who wanted to hurt people. Countless men and women start off well on the leadership journey, but they end badly. They are sabotaged by their blind spots, unaware of their weaknesses. If we want to be a Christian leader, we need to know Christ and be known by Christ.

This means that we can't expect to have the ministry of Jesus and ignore the methods he used. Many Christians try to live a good life while ignoring the way Jesus lived and the empowerment of his Spirit. Leaders will always have people following them — that's nothing special. But good leaders are *learners*. The fact that you are reading this book proves that you have a desire to grow. Every disciple of Jesus Christ should be a learner, and the moment you stop learning, you stop leading.

Jesus was unquestionably the greatest leader to ever walk on planet earth. But *what* made him a great leader? My friend Bill Hull unpacks that question for us, identifying and applying Jesus' leadership-development strategy to life and ministry. He dispels several of the leadership myths that entice both new and seasoned leaders and establishes a biblical standard for effective leadership that is unlike anything taught in today's universities and business schools.

As Bill rightly points out, true Christian leaders celebrate sacrifice, seek humility, and endure hardship — not as a spiritual badge of honor of separation from the pack — but as a natural way of life. They deny themselves, take up their crosses, and follow Christ daily.

What makes Bill's book different from every other leadership book is that he doesn't just explain how to *act like Christ*. He explores how to *be in Christ*. It is our identity in Christ that motivates us to serve Christ in what we do. As Jonathan Edwards proposed in his classic work *Religious Affections*, when our mind's attention is set upon Christ and his word, our heart's affection will follow suit.

This book has been a healing balm to my soul. The chapters "What Makes a Leader Happy" and "Making a Dent in the World" were simultaneously edifying and convicting. If you are like me, you may find yourself pausing as you read to identify and address areas in your life and leadership that need rehabilitation. Come to this book with a receptive heart and allow the Great Physician to perform a deep therapeutic work in your life.

**Robby Gallaty, PhD**
Senior Pastor, Long Hollow Baptist Church
Author of *Growing Up* and *Rediscovering Discipleship*

In the world everyone wants to be a "wolf," and no one is called to play the part of the "sheep." Yet the world cannot *live* without this living witness of sacrifice. That is why ... Christians should be very careful not to be "wolves" ... that is, people who try to dominate others.

Jacques Ellul

# Introduction

Should the leader allow himself to succumb to the wishes of those he leads, who will always seek to turn him into an idol, then the image of the leader will gradually become the image of the misleader. This is the leader who makes an idol of himself and his office and who thus mocks God.

Dietrich Bonhoeffer

**BESIDE MY DESK,** on my desk, and on the bookshelves that surround me are more than seventy-five books on leadership. Over the last year I have read them, scribbled in their margins, underlined passages, and typed what I liked into my research notes. I am not even counting the hundreds of biographies of leaders I have read over the years: evil Mao, funny Mo Udall, confused John Lennon, good John Stott, great Winston Churchill, and mysterious Carl Jung. I have toughed my way through book summaries, YouTube seminars, and personal interviews. I have attended so many seminars on leadership that I can't remember them all. I have led and I have been led. I have a lot of information on leadership theory, skills, and personalities. I have taken the leadership profile assessments, given them to others, and been through the charts, the graphs, and all the "twenty-six ways to be a leader" type of stuff.

Most leadership literature talks about a "right kind" of leadership personality. You know the type: big-picture visionaries who serve others and get the best out of people. They suck all the oxygen out of a room when they enter, and their big smiles reveal their white teeth. They are exciting speakers who move their followers to tears or laughter, as desired.

The question that has nagged me is this: *Did Jesus fit the successful leadership profile?* From everything I know about him, he didn't, nor does he intend or expect that any of us fit the profile. I am writing this book because I believe we need to change how the church views Christian leadership. We have paid homage to a secular model. We have secularized Christian leadership. Now we need to change the way Christians practice leadership.

The word *secular* comes from the Latin *saecularis*, which means "this present world." Its synonyms are *nonreligious*, *profane*, and *temporal* — words associated with humanism, which puts man at the center. It is a worldview that puts God in the margin; he is brought in only to bless humankind's best efforts to achieve. Sadly, many Christian leaders today do not take Jesus seriously when it comes to getting things done in our churches, ministries, and organizations. They look to him for how to pray and what to believe about God, but they don't look to him as a model for how to be a leader. They seem more determined to be like successful secular leaders rather than distinctly Christian in their influence of others. As the late John Stott pointed out, "Leadership is a word shared by Christians and non-Christians alike, but this does not mean that their concept of it is the same."[1] No wonder we have lost the culture.

This is not a book about improving Christian organizations; it is about changing how Christians lead. It is about how rehabilitated leaders change everything they touch. It is for anyone with a megaphone, a platform to speak, who wants to lead others in being a witness for truth. It is for people with a pulpit, whether that pulpit be a business or a position of influence in a domain of the culture: entertainment, sports, politics, industry, the arts, academia, or religion. If you are someone to whom others listen, you have a pulpit—and this book is for you.

We know Jesus as the resurrected King of kings and Lord of lords. I will make my case that he is also our leader and our model for any leading that is to be done in his name. I find Jesus fascinating. He was the smartest, most effective leader in history and yet he didn't seem to try to be a leader, nor did he formally teach others about leadership. He did, however, teach his students to teach others.[2] In this book we will explore how Jesus' style of leadership leads to sacrifice, humility, and suffering. Generations of his disciples labored more than three hundred years in obscurity before achieving a level of power that we today would recognize as important.[3] Jesus had a message and he set his course to deliver it, no matter what. He was a natural leader; he had followers because he influenced people from his person and innate character. Contemporary leaders often don't attain as much.

Most contemporary Christians believe that being noticed in the secular and Christian press is critical to success. It's not that people would state such a belief, but one only has to listen to the excitement generated when some Christian effort is promoted in the press. It is exciting to be noticed, and it is normal to direct future behavior toward getting more notice. After several successful forays into this method of doing what works and getting rewarded, we are hooked. In time, a leadership character is developed in persons, in institutions, and finally in cultures.

This pattern of doing what works and getting rewarded is the enemy of Christian leadership. It thrives on making Christian work impersonal and exploitive. It serves the leader rather than those the leader leads. Sadly, this pattern dominates Christian leadership

17

in the West. It is so powerful that its flow is pulling us along and sometimes under.

I propose that we need a different style of leadership — one patterned after Jesus. We need to learn to influence others out of our character, for that is what Jesus did. He taught us that the key to world revolution is to be yourself in the normal and common parts of life. If this sounds too theoretical for you, let the words of Dallas Willard help you and give you the courage to believe that it can actually be done:

> If [Jesus] were to come today as he did then, he could carry out his mission through most any decent and useful occupation. He could be a clerk or accountant in a hardware store, a computer repairman, a banker, an editor, doctor, waiter, teacher, farmhand, lab technician, or construction worker. He could run a house-cleaning service or repair automobiles. In other words, if he were to come today he could very well do what you do. He could very well live in your apartment or house, hold down your job, have your education and life prospects, and live within your family, surroundings, and time. None of this would be the least hindrance to the eternal kind of life that was his by nature and becomes available to us through him. Our human life, it turns out, is not destroyed by God's life but is fulfilled in it and in it alone.[4]

Jesus influenced others because of *who he was*, not because he was well known or a person of power or because he had mastered a set of skills or implemented an effective leadership strategy. He could have completed his mission living in your house, driving your car, married to your spouse, working at your office, and raising your kids, because leadership comes down to character. Many who aspire to leadership are looking for the right circumstances so they can lead. Many in positions of leadership find it difficult to lead because of obstacles, such as a lack of funds, a lack of authority, or confusion about methods. Jesus faced all of these — and more — yet he accomplished his mission. He said, "Take my yoke upon you and learn from me, for I am gentle and humble in heart, and you will find rest for your souls. For my yoke is easy and my burden is light."[5] Any leader who submits to him and learns from him what it means to lead will be able to lead.

Many have deconstructed the divinity of Christ, the veracity of Christ, the teachings of Christ, and the claims of Christ. I am calling for the deconstruction of the irrelevancy of Christ as a leader. I am calling for the rehabilitation of the Christian leader. Think of reading this work as going into rehab. Rehab normally requires leaving normal routine and committing oneself to a new environment. In this case, you will need to provide your own way of withdrawing from society. It all begins in the mind. The belief that you can feel your way into change is false and dangerous. Knowledge is the starting point. The word *knowledge* in this case is used more broadly than the stimulation of the intellect. It is what we might call an experiential knowing. You begin by reading, then you ponder and meditate on the principles and examples, and then you train yourself to think and act differently.

We will learn from Jesus, from my personal story, and from the examples of leaders such as Winston Churchill and the first-century historian Josephus how to lead and how not to lead.

Underlying it all is the firm foundation of Jesus and his example found in Scripture. Each chapter begins with a title and statement about Jesus' life that will be familiar to many. Regardless of where the book takes you, you will not be far from Christ himself. Jesus was a different kind of teacher. He spoke with a natural authority; it was the nature of his knowledge that set him apart. The Pharisees focused on doing the right thing. Jesus emphasized becoming the kind of person who wants to do the right thing.

Others taught the importance of doing good; Jesus taught how to be good. He didn't teach behavior modification alone; he taught how to change the sources of behavior. It's my hope that you will begin to think of Jesus as your leader. Then you will know what to do with your calling to lead others.

# The Rehabilitation of Christian Leaders

## REHABILITATE YOUR THINKING ABOUT JESUS

"Who do people say I am?"

**Mark 8:27**

The revelation of God in Jesus Christ is something very different from religion.

Peter Berger, *The Precarious Vision*

**THE "REAL WORLD,"** as it often is called, does not take Jesus seriously as a leader. Most people think of him as a mystic or teacher of ethics. They consider him a religious leader of the same ilk as Mother Teresa, the Dalai Lama, or Buddha—someone who attempts to make the world a better place, who inspires people to seek the better angels in our nature and offers some hope for the next life. For many people, Jesus is the kind of leader they pat on the head and say, "You are good for people; we all need a little help; let me make a donation to your cause." They may call upon Jesus for assistance, for wisdom, or for an extra boost, but they don't look to him to solve the world financial crisis. They do not consider the Sermon on the Mount relevant to their work lives. If you want to know quantum physics, Einstein is your man; if you are concerned with origins, Darwin or Gould is the ticket. Jesus is for covering all your bets, to give you someone to talk to as the plane starts rolling toward a takeoff.

Society views Jesus as a teacher, philosopher, and religious person who taught people about the inner life. That is largely where it leaves him—in the church, the monastery, and the Bible study group tucked away in an office behind a closed door during lunch. The decision to not include a prayer at the tenth anniversary memorial ceremony of 9/11 at Ground Zero reflects this separation. To whom the prayer would be addressed is another sign of how tolerance has led to confusion. The resistance is built on a false premise that Jesus speaks only to religious matters and not to public or political life, where life is actually lived.

Over the last fifty years, our perception of the nature of knowledge has changed. Religious knowledge about the soul is no longer

23

on the same level as knowledge about the solar system or genetics. Scientists and other scholars often limit knowledge to what can be proved in a scientific laboratory.[1] Knowledge gained in controlled environments is considered higher and firmer than the knowledge of persons. This split in knowledge is a Faustian deal for the religious world. The university and other societal keepers of knowledge have said, "We will take knowledge," and told the church, "You take faith." And by obediently stepping aside, we Christians have sold our collective soul for a place, albeit a benign place, at the table. It is the chaplain's syndrome—the religious "expert" asked to open or close meetings with prayer, or the priest on the team sideline who is little more than a good-luck charm.

Clearly, it is not the non-Christian world alone that needs to be convinced that Jesus is competent as a world-class leader; Christians also need convincing. There is a great gulf between honoring Jesus as God and Savior of the world and seeing him as someone who is competent to help with tough decisions. I saw this split in a good friend of mine. His first prayer in the courtroom as a Christian lawyer was *I love you, Lord, but I would appreciate it if you would just stay out of this legal proceeding. I've got this.* My friend's attitude is common. Many Christians think that Jesus is qualified to help them in their spiritual lives but question whether he understands or would even bother to take an interest in the rest of their lives, whether in a courtroom or office or kitchen. Peter had to make this decision when Jesus asked him to cast the nets out again after he and his fellow fishermen had failed to catch any fish all night long. Peter decided that this out-of-work carpenter had knowledge about fishing because of who he was.[2] Jesus had capacities that made him an expert on everything.

The question for the church is this: Are we going to settle for marginalization and allow Jesus to live in the margins with us? Let's not forget that Jesus can be marginalized only in his official capacity as the head of the visible church; he will insist on continuing his work in the world, even if he must do so unaccompanied by his own people. Let's follow him into the fray and learn from him about how to lead others. After all, Jesus is the only person who can be completely trusted and followed as a leader.

# Uniquely Qualified: Fully Divine, Fully Human

Some people abuse the word *unique* by placing the adjective *very* before it. *Unique* means one of a kind, so it can't be "very" anything. But if a reason existed to abuse it, Jesus would be that reason. Consider the words of sociologist Peter Berger at the start of the chapter: "The revelation of God in Jesus Christ is something very different from religion." Berger introduced the point that Jesus is something above and beyond conventional religion. The Bible itself claims, "The Son is the image of the invisible God, the firstborn over all creation. For in him all things were created: things in heaven and on earth, visible and invisible."[3]

I read recently about a subatomic particle called a neutrino. Experiments in 2011 suggested it traveled a nanosecond faster than the speed of light. Although refuted months later, this discovery had the scientific community in a whirl; we were told it meant something important. When Jesus was walking the earth, did he know about the neutrino? If he created all things, even the things unseen, then of course he did. As the creator and manager of all creation, he is greater than any philosophy or organized religious body. "He is before all things," Paul asserted, "and in him all things hold together."[4]

This suggests that Jesus is unique and holds a preeminent and special place with regard to all people and things. Scripture also claims that he will someday reconcile all things to himself.[5] The smartest people on earth were baffled by the world financial crisis.

25

They are at a loss as to how to resolve ancient conflicts over land erupting from tribal and religious differences. Scripture tells us that Christ will someday return to the earth and solve all our problems. Under him, his followers will live harmoniously in a new heaven and new earth. If Jesus is able to do all that, then certainly he can help you run your dry-cleaning business.

If you believe in the Christian doctrine of the incarnation, that Jesus is God in human flesh, then you must believe Jesus was the smartest person who ever lived. He grew up in a small village in a normal family with siblings and was trained to be a carpenter by his father. As a twelve-year-old, Jesus astonished the elders in the temple with his knowledge, but he never became an official scholar or a rabbinical student.[6] He grew in wisdom and in stature and in favor with God and all the people. He would have been put on the fast track to rabbinical fame, but somehow he avoided such a fate, which would have made his mission impossible. You can't be an outsider by being an insider. Jesus' father, Joseph, died sometime after Jesus was twelve and before he began his ministry at age thirty. This could have played a role in why Jesus didn't move to Jerusalem to pursue studies in official Judaism. His obligations to his mother and younger siblings would have taken priority.

Consider for a moment what life may have been like for Jesus. He was fully human, so he would have felt and experienced life as we do. He likely arose early six days a week to work as a carpenter. Growing up, he would have learned the trade from his father; after his father's death, he would have trained his brothers how to do carpentry work. Jesus ate, slept, got childhood diseases, felt under the weather, injured his hands with tools, developed calluses, and grew weary — the same as the rest of us. He argued with his brothers and sisters and negotiated with his mother. He did business with his neighbors and was attracted to women. As he matured, the awareness of his life's mission also grew within him. Part of what made — and makes — Jesus worthy of our trust is the faithfulness, discipline, and patience he exhibited in the thirty years of his private life.

Ironically, if asked to critique Jesus' life, many modern leaders and advisers of future leaders would consider much of Jesus' twenties wasted time. After all, they would say, think how much more he would have accomplished if he had started earlier, moved to Jerusalem, became known, and developed a network among the influential!

Additionally, a growing number of skeptical scholars are on a newly fueled mission to erase the Jesus of the Bible from history. They don't like what they read about Jesus in the biblical texts, so they have attacked the documents and gone in search of a more accommodating fellow they call "the historical Jesus." The quest for the historical Jesus has largely presented a demythologized man absent of miracles and claims of divinity. The quest has been led by skeptics and doubters who want to give the world a Jesus they can believe in without faith — someone to admire but not worship. This Jesus taught kindness but failed to get through to the religious leaders of his day and was tragically killed. He left behind wonderful principles which, if adopted, would make the world less violent and people more caring. But he won't be coming back; he won't be solving our problems. He won't be back, because he is dead.

This mission to erase the Jesus of the Bible from history is new only in the way that the printing press is new or the telephone or electricity is new. Many skeptics start by dismissing the New Testament as a serious document of antiquity. They cannot honestly do this, of course, if they apply the same test to the New Testament as they do to other historical documents. They seem eager to accept Vedic myths, the Upanishads, or the Bhagavad Gita. But then, why wouldn't they? None of the mystic religions challenge their authority with a personal God who must be obeyed!

27

Jesus not only made demands on all people's lives, he claimed much more. His claims were absolute, universal in scope, and outrageous in their implications. When confronted by the scholars of his day as to his identity and right to speak with such authority, Jesus spoke with such ferocity that it sent his questioners into conniptions: "'Very truly I tell you,' Jesus answered, 'before Abraham was born, I am!' At this, they picked up stones to stone him, but Jesus hid himself, slipping away from the temple grounds."[7] When Philip asked Jesus to show him and the other disciples the Father, Jesus' reaction was equally strong. At the Last Supper he told his disciples, "Don't you know me, Philip, even after I have been among you such a long time? Anyone who has seen me has seen the Father. How can you say, 'Show us the Father'? Don't you believe that I am in the Father, and that the Father is in me?"[8] Jesus also commended Peter when his most verbose disciple "nailed it," identifying him as the Messiah:

> "But what about you?" he asked. "Who do you say I am?" Simon Peter answered, "You are the Messiah, the Son of the living God." Jesus replied, "Blessed are you, Simon son of Jonah, for this was not revealed to you by flesh and blood, but by my Father in heaven."[9]

Jesus simply does not give us middle ground; anyone who made the claims he made would be either a liar or exactly who he said he was. C. S. Lewis is famous for saying that Jesus was a legend, a lunatic, a liar, or God. I am prepared to say that based on the evidence, Jesus clearly was not a legend or a lunatic. Sociologist Rodney Stark summarized why the quest for the historical Jesus ends with the conclusion that Jesus actually did exist:

> There is no sure evidence outside of the New Testament scriptures that Jesus actually lived. But all reputable scholars

now agree that the Gospel evidence is sufficient, not because the Bible is authoritative, but because it clearly reflects the common culture of first-generation Christians — their behavior makes absolutely no sense if there was no Jesus. To deny that Jesus existed it is necessary to claim that the entire New Testament was made up at a later date. However, no one competent now doubts that most of Paul's letters were authentic.[10]

Smart people follow Plato, Socrates, or Aristotle. They read their works and preach their philosophies, but they know less about them than we do about Jesus. Evidence also demonstrates that Jesus was cogent in his thoughts and able to interact with people. He was considered normal in the most foundational of ways. So I think it is most likely that he was either a liar or who he said he was.

So, was he a liar? It is ironic to think that one of the world's great moral teachers would lie about the main tenet of his teaching, namely, that he was God's Son come to save the world.[11] Is it possible that Jesus was a cunning, slippery man who was able to arrange to have himself executed for his lie and to have his body secretly removed so that he would live on in the minds and hearts of his duped followers? For such a plan to work, he would have needed to find people who were not his followers to help him pull it off, as his disciples obviously knew nothing about it. We know they knew nothing because they willingly died for him. After they lived and suffered for him, they were crucified, beheaded, and burned alive. This was an incredible change in character, since they had abandoned him in fear at his arrest in Gethsemane. If his resurrection was all a lie, why didn't any of them just say, "Okay, the gig is up. Let me tell you how we did it." His disciples chose to follow him for one reason only: They knew he was alive. After his resurrection from the dead they had touched him, talked with him, worshipped with him, and were commissioned by him.[12] There is no other reasonable or logical explanation for how they spent the rest of their lives. An unprejudiced historian would be hard-pressed not to agree. Even the most hardened atheistic scientist claims to know his children and would consider his inner feelings irrefutable evidence of who they are. And in that larger laboratory of knowledge that includes knowledge of persons, Jesus is uniquely qualified to be a leader, for he changed ordinary men filled with fear and doubt into courageous zealots who changed history. As God, Jesus is the perfect model for leadership because he knows everything that is to be known about it. Can you think of a stronger qualification for a leader? I cannot.

Oddly enough, Jesus' own followers present the best argument for why not to take him seriously. After all, skeptical scholars have an agenda. They intend to spoil the biblical portrayal of Jesus. They don't believe, and they don't want anyone else to believe. His own followers, however, have no such intention. They intend to convince others that indeed Jesus is the Christ, the one to follow and to worship, but their methods sabotage their message.

## The Church Is in Trouble

American evangelicals who are aggressive both in evangelism and in political work have at times allowed their theological convictions to be expressed in a rigid, judgmental way. Granted, a skeptical press has caricatured them, but evangelicals must own our responsibility in this regard. Evangelism or personal witness has become depicted as Christians bothering people. People in general don't want to hear the gospel message, and under present conditions most Christians don't want to share it. I recently heard someone say, "In many places in the world the church is persecuted and fears the raised fist. In America, the church is not persecuted and fears the raised eyebrow." We hesitate because we don't like to be characterized as bigots, racists, or uneducated buffoons. In some cases, we have earned this reputation.

Evangelical leaders have used Jesus as a blunt instrument, a battering ram of truth; after having repeatedly thumped him into the resistant wall of secularism, we point to the dents and call it progress. We have failed to assimilate the person and teachings of Jesus into the general culture because our approaches have often been formal and frontal.[13] The most aggressive wing of the church has given people a choice: "Commit yourself to Jesus and receive eternal life, or reject Jesus and go to hell." Many Americans, it seems, have decided to take their chances on hell. And why not? They don't like what they see in evangelical churches and in Christians. Why should you stake your future on an organization that is dying and a group of people about whom you have concluded, "I don't want to be like them or with them"?

The church is in trouble. This is obvious from the primary way we gauge spiritual interest: church attendance. It is not the correct way to assess spiritual interest, but for the moment we will measure by the numbers. Yes, many people say they are "spiritual" but not "religious." What this means, however, is that they want to be good but don't want to submit to authority, so they use the word *spiritual*, which means nothing. In 2005 pollster George Barna found that 47% of American adults attend church on a typical weekend. But in 2008 David T. Olson's more in-depth analysis rocked the American church when he reported the figure was actually 17.5%. His American Church Research Project broke that figure down to 9.1% evangelical, 3.0% mainline (mostly churches of moderate or liberal theology), and 5.3% Catholic. The slow but steady decline in church attendance continues.[14]

The prognosis is that the church will continue to decline gradually and will fall far short of staying up with population growth.

And most of the loss will be among younger adults. Another way to view this decline is from the evangelical standpoint. The evangelical church, which by all accounts both in experience and in research is the most vibrant wing of American Christianity, is in decline and weakened.

The Barna Group identified six trends or "megathemes" that emerged from its 2010 research on the American church:

1. The Christian church is becoming less theologically literate.

2. Christians are becoming more ingrown and less outreach-oriented.

3. Growing numbers of people are less interested in spiritual principles and more desirous of learning pragmatic solutions for life.

4. Among Christians, interest in participating in community action is escalating.

5. The postmodern insistence on tolerance is winning over the Christian church.

6. The influence of Christianity on culture and individual lives is largely invisible.[15]

Megathemes 5 and 6 present the greatest concern. The inability of the church to manage the need to seem tolerant while holding to moral absolutes has made Christians hesitant to speak up, take a stand, and stake out moral boundaries. The irony of such compromise is that the church is not now as well respected by its foes, and ground has been lost instead of gained. The church appears to be weak and flagging; it no longer serves its communities as a bulwark of stability, the bastion of ancient truth.

Barna wrote, "In a period of history where image is reality, and life-changing decisions are made on the basis of such images, the

Christian Church is in desperate need of a more positive and accessible image.... The solution is not solely providing an increase in preaching and public relations."[16] He went on to say that American culture today is driven by snap judgments made amid busy schedules and with incomplete information. So it should come as no surprise that the influence of the church and its members is nearly invisible. What people think of Christians on this basis is not fair, but impressions never have been.

The research confirmed that whatever the church is focusing on, it isn't working. The problem is simple to define: *The American church is not producing mature leaders and followers of Christ who are vibrant, mature, and engaged with their neighbors and communities. The evidence is plainly before us.* This problem won't be fixed overnight, but the work to fix it must begin now. Barna wrote: "How [the Christian] responds to life's opportunities and challenges [is what] most substantially [shapes] people's impressions of and interest in Christianity."[17] Christ's disciples need to live convincing lives that persuade non-Christians to become Christian. John Wesley eloquently summarized what the church needs to be producing His questioner was precise.[18]

> "I hear that you preach to a great number of people every night and morning. Pray, what would you do with them? Whither would you lead them? What religion do you preach? What good is it for?" ...
>
> Wesley replied, "I do preach to as many as desire to hear, every night and morning. You ask, what would I do with them: I would make them virtuous and happy, easy in themselves and useful to others. Whither would I lead them? To heaven; to God the Judge, the lover of all, and to Jesus the mediator of the New Covenant. What religion do I preach? The religion of love; the law of kindness brought to light by the gospel. What is it good for? To make all who receive it

enjoy God and themselves: to make them all like God; lovers of all; contented in their lives; and crying out at their death, in calm assurance, 'O grave, where is thy victory! Thanks be unto God, who giveth me the victory through my Lord Jesus Christ.' "[19]

Christian leaders must pay urgent attention to persuading docile Christians to take up the life of discipleship. For the truth is that five hundred awakened Christians are far more powerful than five hundred new Christians. This is only true, however, when intentional apprenticeship is taken up, because then multiplication is possible.

The problem may be approached in many ways, but I believe the fix begins with leadership. Christian leaders must be convinced that following the ways and means of Jesus is superior to, and in the long run more effective than, attractive secular models. At the end of the next decade, a significant start can be had; in twenty years, a real turnaround is doable. The problem, however, is buried deeply in the church and in the culture. So the rehabilitation process will require repentance, a conscious turning away from trust in the pragmatism of what "works" to a commitment to learn how to relate to others as Jesus did. The American church is in trouble, but Jesus is not in trouble. His ways and means are not in trouble, and his call to us to live and work like him is not in trouble. It all is easily accessible to any interested person. If Christian leaders can be rehabilitated to recognize that Jesus is a relevant model in character and conduct for living in the real world, there is hope.

# Leading as Jesus Did

Consider the contrast between the way Herod led and the way Jesus led. Herod lived for himself; Jesus lived for others. Herod derived his influence via power and terror. He had his wife and two sons killed to consolidate power. His behavior prompted Caesar Augustus to say, "I would rather be Herod's pig than his son."[20] Jesus' influence, however, was based on his character and on his living out the tenets he taught in the Sermon on the Mount. His influence was his personal power, which he presented as a result of his special connection to his Father.[21]

The challenge for the Christian leader is to find the same balance Jesus found. He had enough ambition to carry out his mission and enough humility to stay in submission to his Father. He knew when to back off, when not to take the bait or go for the shortcut that would abort his mission. Satan tried to get him to abandon his path to the cross; so did Peter, so did the Jewish leaders, and so did his own humanness. History would turn on his decisions; Jesus did it his own way, unlike most Christian leaders today. Jesus said he was the way, the truth, and the life.[22] Indeed, he had a way of leading; his way was the means by which he conducted his life and how he treated people.

I might add that Jesus crammed a lot into a little over three years of public ministry—less than one US presidential term. He wasn't in a hurry; he wasn't racked with anxiety, and his ambitions didn't conform to the political or religious climate. Yet he became the centerpiece of human history. He has billions of followers, and the book written about him remains the all-time best seller. He leads the world's largest organization. I think we should pay attention to how he did it. His way was personal and ran contrary to the dominant leadership model. Eugene Peterson wrote, "We cannot use impersonal means to do or say a personal thing—and the gospel is personal or it is nothing."[23] Christ was willing to sacrifice the immediate spoils of success to get long-term results. He left with eleven followers, but now he has billions. Very few leaders are willing to make that sacrifice; we want results now.

# Will It Really Make a Difference?

Perhaps you are wondering whether it will make a difference if we as Christian leaders change our thoughts and behavior about how to lead. The answer is determined by the goal. If by rehabilitated leaders we mean rehabilitated pastors, then the objective is narrowed to local congregations. The answer would be yes—pastors with new ways of thinking and behaving can change the ethos of their congregations. In fact, pastors are the single best hope for setting into motion the movement that will spur the church to accomplish what it should: to make disciples of all people.[24] Churches are to be outposts in the larger world and the places where Christians are taught and trained so they can be useful in making disciples.

The church and its leaders have always been on the margins of society, not at the cultural center. The president of a Christian denomination does not have the same societal influence as the president of Harvard or Stanford. An article in the *New York Times* or *Wall Street Journal* is more widely distributed than the same in the *Moline Dispatch*. Because of this, some think that the church should be intentional about reaching leaders who have cultural influence. Cultural elites make the important decisions about government and major educational and cultural institutions, and the only way Christians can change society is to convert the leaders who count. But will such a strategy work, and is it the one that Christian leaders are commissioned to undertake? I don't believe so. The genius of God's method of bringing people into his kingdom is that we don't get to be part of the selection committee. God is at work in many a person's heart, both before and after a decision to follow Christ.

Dallas Willard spoke to this in a way that can startle the contemporary mind-set:

Ministers pay far too much attention to people who do *not* come to services. Those people should, generally, be given exactly that disregard by the pastor that they gave to Christ. The Christian leader has something much more important to do than pursue the godless. The leader's task is to *equip saints until they are like Christ* (Eph. 4:12), and history and the God of history waits for him to do *this* job.[25]

Every church has two categories of leaders. The first are pastors and teachers, whose primary role is to equip people for ministry. The second are leaders whose primary venue is the workplace and in the community. *If the first set does its job, those in the second group can do theirs.* Church leaders are called to train and deploy the entire congregation, regardless of gifts or status, so that they infiltrate society and live and work with those who need Christ. Our goal is to fill the culture with people who exhibit the character of Christ and influence people the way Jesus did.

# To Reach or to Change the World?

I heard a sermon recently that called Christians to change the world, to take it over in the power and authority of Jesus. I don't believe this is our calling, responsibility, or the purpose of the Great Commission. In fact, Andy Crouch, in his book *Culture Making*, pointed out that "changing the world" talk is relatively new to Christian literature. He and Nate Barksdale searched the Harvard University library system for all books and titles that included the phrases "change the world," "changing the world" or "changed the world." There were 216 results; seventy-five were published after 2000. Another 101 were published in the previous decade. Eighteen were published in the 1980s, four in the 1970s, eight in the 1960s, and four in the 1950s. A total of six were published in the fifty years before that. Crouch delivered the punch line: "Of the 1.5 million titles in the Harvard collections published before 1900, how many included a reference to changing the world? Zero."[26]

There are a number of ways to draw meaning from such studies. I suppose one could conclude that because we think more globally today, global matters are a greater concern. We know more about hunger, disease, and war around the world and it is easier to publish our thoughts; everyone can be a writer via social networks, available to anyone who cares to comment. The other factor is hubris. Because we know about the world, we are more likely to think we can change it.

The world is harder to change than most religious leaders think. In his excellent work on the Crusades, *God's Battalions*, sociologist Rodney Stark pointed out how long it took for a conquered nation to thoroughly change its religion. He found that it took an average of 250 years for a Christian nation to become half Muslim.[27] This is apparent when one drives through Istanbul, Turkey. It was once the center of the Christian world, but now minarets of Islamic mosques dominate the skyline. The same is true of many other Muslim countries. These countries did not change because of missionary work or proselytizing. They changed because war and conquest forced a new religion and way of life upon them, but it took on average more than two centuries for each country to change from an official Muslim country to a genuine Muslim country, where most of the general populace practiced the religion.

The New Testament calls Christians not to military conquest but to a divine conspiracy of disciples making other disciples. We are told: "This gospel of the kingdom will be preached in the whole world as a testimony to all nations, and then the end will come."[28] The end that Jesus spoke of is the return of Christ, and it will trigger the kind of actions that will truly change the world into paradise.[29] In the meantime, Christ's followers are charged to be disciples, to make other disciples, to love one another, and to love the world—that is all we need to do. The church's calling is to send a transformed people into the living spaces of society and to establish a presence: the presence of Christ in every facet of a community.

# Pushing and Pulling

Some things by nature can be pushed but not pulled, like keys on a keyboard. Other things can be pulled but not pushed, which would include most people. Leaders cannot push people into world revolution, but we can pull them into it by our example. The determining factor is whether we model Jesus' style of leadership. When these leaders say, "Follow me," people will do so because they see leaders they want to follow.

# What Makes a Leader Happy?

## REHABILITATE YOUR MOTIVATION

Make my joy complete by being like-minded, having the same love, being one in spirit and of one mind.

Philippians 2:2

The world is my oyster.

William Shakespeare,
*The Merry Wives of Windsor*

**AS A YOUNG LEADER,** I wanted those I led to work on whatever I put in their minds, and I wanted them to succeed in our projects so that I would get my needs met. I hadn't claimed the world as my oyster, but certainly the church was. It was mine to consume and use to meet my need for significance. Did I know this? Of course not. I would have laughed at you if you had suggested it. I would have denied it and would not have believed it.

After all, I was committed to evangelism; I organized outreach events and provided training for church members. My church was very successful. We attracted many seekers, and many made decisions to follow Christ. I encouraged our people to be mindful about whom they talked to and invited to our events. I recommended that they work only with those who were candidates to attend our church. I didn't think it did much good to lead people to Christ who would attend another church. I had attendance goals I wanted to reach.

If I was not seeing enough progress numerically, an inner pressure would build inside me over time. This would invariably lead to a passionate burst of emotion and a "get with the program" type of sermon. In one of my "best" I said something like, "I don't know about you, but I am tired of playing church. I want to see some new Christians around here. If you are as fed up as I am with dinking around, meet me this afternoon at two o'clock, and we will go door-to-door in this community for Christ." I went home and after lunch I asked my wife, Jane, if she was going with me to the church to do the door-to-door thing. She looked at me with a little smile. "No, I would rather have my arms amputated," she said. In the end, I don't think even I went. She convinced me that no one would show up.

I cared about people, I was sincere, and I was highly motivated for Christ. I had lofty hopes and dreams. Like Thor Heyerdahl standing gallantly on the bow of his raft *Kon-Tiki,* I stared out to sea with a confident smirk, knowing that just over the horizon were great opportunities, more adventure, and worlds to conquer. Heyerdahl could not swim; neither did I appreciate the peril I was in. I was happy when those I respected noticed and affirmed me as a leader. (That still makes me happy, by the way.) Today, however, the primary source of my happiness as a leader is similar to Paul's, who told the church at Philippi, "Make my joy complete by being like-minded, having the same love, being one in spirit and of one mind."[1]

Paul prefaced this statement by saying, "Is there any encouragement from belonging to Christ? Any comfort from his love? Any fellowship together in the Spirit? Are your hearts tender and compassionate?"[2] In other words, it made Paul happy when those around his followers could see that being a disciple was useful for life. He found his greatest joy in other people's success. I feel the same.

Getting to this place took many years and several transitions. I want to describe them to you, because if we are going to learn to lead like Jesus, most of us need to go through a similar process.

# First Transition: From Seeking Recognition to Learning to Act Caringly

I was a new pastor, about one year into it, and some people in the congregation started complaining that I was cold, uncaring, and aloof. The truth was that I was shy, socially awkward, and tall. I was also driven to succeed, to make things happen, and I had the theology to back it up: "We are to be and make disciples,"[3] beginning in our home area and working our way out to the world. I believed that everything else was a sideshow, a waste of time — what Pascal called "licking the earth."[4]

One of my favorite sayings was, "Discipleship is the name of the game; it's the only game in town. If you are here for any other reason, I am not sure why you are here. We are not here for the music; we are not here to socialize; we are not here to see our friends; we are here to get trained, equipped. You are soldiers, warriors. Otherwise, stay home, play golf, watch TV, putter around in your garage. Don't waste your time here." I am sure there was a mean look on my red face and that people were slumping in their chairs, trying not to get burned by my fiery darts.

The complaints spread, and I went to my superintendent to find out what to do. I told him about the progress that was being made but that some in the church were unhappy with me. He said, "I know about the complaints. I have had several calls." He saw that I was angry and said, "Bill, they are just afraid that you might push them right out of the church. They don't think you care about them." He went on to explain what I should do: "Next week when you complete your sermon, tell the congregation that you know that some believe you are cold, uncaring, and aloof. Ask them to help you learn to love and to communicate how you really feel toward others." I was appalled. "I can't say that! They will think I have a problem," I sputtered. He looked at me with a smile and said, "Bill, they already know you have a problem. I promise you that if you tell them you are sorry and that you want their help, they will come out of the woodwork to affirm you."

So that Sunday I did as he recommended. I even said, "Would you help me learn to love?" My mentor was a prophet. The congregation embraced me. For the next few years, the church coached me in good humor about how to act caringly. It was a turning point because they helped me and I was better able to help them. How?

By trusting that God would work in them and by recognizing that they wanted what I wanted, a vibrant life in Christ. I found freedom in understanding that they would not necessarily go about it the same way I would.

Here's a case in point. One day I asked a church member to go door-to-door with me in the neighborhood, and we visited a man who was unusually rude. He answered the door and said, "What?" He was obviously annoyed by our presence. I introduced ourselves and said that we were so glad his wife had visited our church the previous Sunday. He shot back, "Look, I don't care what my wife did. I don't need any of that!" After a few more choice words, he slammed the door in our faces. This encounter was not what the church member wanted or expected. He was shaken. I needed to realize that sheep normally don't go to war; they don't do daring things. I had to rethink how I might help them.

I am still learning how to love and care for others. It is a daily quest rooted in the soil of everyday life. Will I empty the dishwasher for my wife? Will I invite to lunch a lonely person who can't help me in any way? Yes, this transition is long, but there are milestones, those moments we remember when something important changed.

# Second Transition: From Focusing on Me to Focusing on Others

Let's look at a familiar passage on transformation:

> So we tell others about Christ, warning everyone and teaching everyone with all the wisdom God has given us. We want to present them to God, perfect in their relationship to Christ. That's why I work and struggle so hard, depending on Christ's mighty power that works within me.[5]

The words that jump off the page at me are "present them to God." One of Paul's great strengths as a leader was that he considered people's attitude and conduct the central focus of his work; he was an artist presenting his work to God. Paul was clear. Leaders are to grow from being focused on how they are feeling and doing to being focused on how to lead their followers to maturity. According to him, the task of bringing others to spiritual maturity requires hard work, work that God alone is able to do through us.

I am not sure exactly when I became focused on others. Many experiences played a role. One watershed moment was the day I sat down with one of my sons and asked, "How did you experience me as a father?" He told me that he learned right and wrong from me, that I was a good model of a Christian father, but that we weren't very close. What he meant was that we didn't have a lot of common interests. His answer shook me. It told me what I had to own up to. I had related to my son as if he were a project, just like my other projects. For me, being a good father was a duty, a goal to check off my list. I was more interested in making sure my son turned out "good" than I was in enjoying him. This conversation didn't take place until I was fifty years old; it causes me to wince as I write.

The transition of learning to focus on others instead of ourselves is treacherous emotionally because it requires that we own up to our influence on others. It causes us to ask, "If the people around me are afraid, am I afraid? Am I acting in a way that causes them to be afraid? If they are sour of spirit, did I create it? If they are positive, was I the model?"

I saw with my son that I needed a new way to evaluate my life and impact. Christian leaders also need new standards of measurement for gauging success. I like the metrics that Harvard University professor Dr. Clayton M. Christensen recommends. He teaches a course on humility and has his students ask themselves three questions: (1) How can I be sure that I will be happy in my career? (2) How can I be sure that my relationships with my spouse and my family become an enduring source of happiness? (3) How can I be sure I'll stay out of jail?[6]

The last question is not frivolous for a graduate of Harvard Business School or for any leader. Professor Christensen suggests that leaders take one hour per day reading, thinking, and praying about why God put them on this earth. He credits this habit in the middle of his heavy schedule as a Rhodes scholar as the reason he figured out the purpose of his life.

Your true purpose dictates what you measure to determine whether you are successful. For example, early in my ministry my stated purpose was to reach the world for Christ, but what I measured was church attendance. My true purpose was a larger congregation, not reaching the world for Christ. By changing the world, I meant making disciples who reproduce, but my measurable goal was putting more people in the seats via my preaching.

Church size is not the optimum metric for Christian leaders; the standard needs to be mature followers of Christ who act like Christ Monday through Saturday in the ordinary places of life (as well as on Sunday!). This does not mean, however, that pastors of large churches or captains of industry are not following the right metrics; size is incidental and is more a product of talent, personality, circumstances, innovation, and skill. Actually, those who lack recognition are most desperate for it and most susceptible to such a temptation.

Paul was able to define what made him happy. He rejoiced when the people he influenced and taught became mature followers of Christ and when they lived and worked together in harmony and were Christlike in the world.[7] If Christian leaders measure those things, it won't make our work easier, but it will make it different. We are then committed to quality of persons, rather than quantity.

# Third Transition: From Valuing Numbers to Valuing the End Result

One day I was fed up. I left the office in the middle of the day and didn't tell my staff where I was going. No one was home and I sat down on the couch and started listing what I could do besides being a pastor. The list included basketball coach, FBI agent, police officer, insurance salesman, and so on. After a few phone calls I realized that my training and experience did not make me a likely candidate for anything other than being a pastor. I returned to the office the next day, knowing that if I didn't intentionally change the way I was leading the church, I would badly misspend my life. I decided I should take the following actions, for only actions matter. They are not ambiguous. I decided to take three steps.

First, I decided to quit teaching a Bible study on Wednesday nights, composed of veteran church members, and to start a group in my home for newcomers. This action would give me ten weeks to get to know people who were ready to become apprentices of Jesus. Just to alert you, such decisions are not without a price. There was a reaction, but I cleared the decision with those who attended the sessions; they gave me their blessing. I also cleared the decision with our governing body; they also gave me their blessing. The class was usually attended by fifteen to twenty people; the following Wednesday evening more than seventy-five nonclass members crammed into the chapel in protest. It was enough to confirm that I had made the right decision.

Second, I decided to concentrate on younger leaders who were hungry to be trained. I had to create a system in which leaders could be identified, trained in that system, and then become teachers in that system. I also had to select leaders who would be willing to meet at 5:00 a.m. once a week. We formed a group of young men who could argue, learn, and work together for a common cause. By the way, 5:00 a.m. meetings tend to keep away the spiritual riffraff. By week three, the willing are with you and the unwilling are slobbering into their pillows.

Finally, I decided to be a disciple-making pastor and start writing about Jesus being a disciple maker. Writing would give me opportunity to think through my ideas and practices. It would also provide material for those I was training and for other leaders who had similar interests.

I made these decisions in 1982; they set my course and have resulted in a meaningful way of life. I have been a voice for discipleship among leaders and their followers around the world. Subsequent crucial turning points have prompted me to refocus my life, but the metrics haven't changed. I still count disciples.

Of course, just because you change actions and get new results doesn't mean you will be happy. I know this because of two things that happened between 1981 and 1984. The first was that I trained a group of about ten men. I spent time with them and taught them how to lead, teach, and, most importantly, think about the world and our role in it. It was a dream come true for me, and those ten men affected hundreds of others then and have affected thousands by now. The second thing was that I was engaged in a spiritual war with various factions in the congregation. The political infighting was intense. People were organizing a rebellion, and my family was attacked. It was a miserable existence.

One night in January 1984 I decided I had to get out of there, and a few weeks later I resigned from the church. I had changed my actions and brought about new results, but I can't say that I was a happy man. I had been fulfilled in my work with my young leaders; it was the highlight of my week. I loved studying, writing, preaching, and doing pastoral things, but the infighting soured my soul. The reason I left was simple. I could choose to leave and so I did. I would need to learn to stay the course somewhere else the next time.

# Fourth Transition:
# From Leading from the Outside
# to Leading from the Inside

When I looked at my staff and at the members of our church, I confess that I never went where Clayton Christensen went in his mind. He put himself into the minds and lives of his employees. In an article for *Harvard Business Review*, he wrote:

> In my mind's eye I saw one of my managers leave for work one morning with a relatively strong level of self-esteem. Then I pictured her driving home to her family 10 hours later, feeling unappreciated, frustrated, underutilized, and demeaned. I imagined how profoundly her lowered self-esteem affected the way she interacted with her children. The vision in my mind then fast-forwarded to another day when she drove home with greater self-esteem — feeling that she had learned a lot, been recognized for achieving valuable things, and played a significant role in the success of some important initiatives. I then imagined how positively that affected her as a spouse and a parent.[8]

Reading this article brought to mind a woman in my congregation who had four sons. One Sunday I was upset with her for accusing me of being too dominant as a leader and saying that God was no longer working through me. I referred to her attitude in a sermon, saying that such judgmental attitudes made me want to "throw up." (You know, just as Jesus said he would spew the Laodicean church out of his mouth.) I didn't mention her name, but the woman knew I was talking about her. After the sermon she approached me and told me that she no longer wanted her sons to be exposed to me and that I created turmoil in her home. She did not want her sons imitating my bitterness and anger. Reflecting on that situation, I regret what I created in her home. The content of my spirit revealed my character. Spiritual power is not domination; it is not based in anger and revenge.

I began to ask myself how my actions and the environment I created as a leader affected those in my church, both employees and church members. After all, how they treated their families when they went home could be influenced by what they experienced during the day. It struck me that my first responsibility as a leader was to be a good example. I was beginning to see that as a Christian leader my task is to help others do Christian things, whether they recognize them as Christian or not. But being a good example was not something I could manufacture. People around me would know if I was authentic. I needed to become the kind of person who would actually *be* what I wanted others to be.

Henri Nouwen's book *In the Name of Jesus: Reflections on Christian Leadership* gave me a pathway for how I could begin to lead out of my character, out of who I was.[9] Nouwen identified three changes that need to take place in this transformation process. We need to move from relevance to prayer, from the spectacular to the ordinary, and from leading to being led. Let me summarize and comment on what he said about each of these.

## From Relevance to Prayer

Being relevant is a big temptation in a leader's life. People expect leaders to be up-to-date, even ahead of their time. Being relevant is particularly dangerous for younger leaders who are hip and full of new ideas. When leaders with charisma and talent rise fast, they find themselves surrounded by a spiritual entourage that enables them and can keep them suspended in a spiritual adolescence. This explains why it is common to find people over fifty who still throw temper tantrums and treat those around them with disdain. This kind of behavior is bad enough when seen in a young leader who suddenly comes into money and fame, but it is heartbreaking to see in leaders as they grow older. The list is long of people who were ruined by money, fame, and the need to be relevant. The danger of success is that it can give birth to arrested development.

To be relevant, a Christian leader must be able to communicate with others so that they can find God, appreciate his beauty, and experience the life he has planned for us. But Christian leaders shouldn't make relevance their goal. To chase after relevance is to chase the wind; relevance and fame keep giving us the slip. The skeptical reader might think, *Ah, leaders who are not relevant and don't speak to the culture are the ones who want to escape to a life of prayer.* This certainly cannot be said of Henri Nouwen. He was an unconventional Catholic priest who experienced a good deal of fame. He taught at Notre Dame, Harvard, and Yale. Millions read his books. He left teaching in the Ivy League, however, to care for a disabled man in a community in Canada. He realized that being famous and relevant had led to vanity, so he left the limelight and chose a life of prayer.

Like most driven leaders, I've been tempted by relevance. I, like Nouwen, have chosen the prayer road and have found it as difficult as anything I have ever undertaken. Nothing will test your faith more than to pray and then sit back and wait for God to act. The test for leaders is not whether we will pray alone or whether we will retreat with others to pray and listen to God. What matters is in what realm we will pray. For example, many business leaders are willing to go on retreats with their pastors for a time of prayer about their ministry as a church. Those same leaders, however, won't relinquish control and results of their own work to God, for it is the place to which they look to get their need for worth and significance met. They have not let go of the need to be relevant; that need is still being met in their work life. I don't think Christian leaders can be happy until they release control of what they lead.

And letting go must be thought about contemplatively for

many hours of the day, not just as an item on our prayer list. Prayer needs to be a frame of mind, a trajectory of thought. Living among and serving broken, wounded, and unpretentious people forced Nouwen to let go of the relevant self that was an intellectual force, a prestigious writer, a man put on a pedestal by millions — "the self that can do things, show things, prove things, build things — and forced me to reclaim that unadorned self in which I am completely vulnerable, open to receive and give love regardless of any accomplishments."[10] Nouwen was happy; for him, happiness had been reduced to the giving and receiving of love. When all the relevance issues were gone from his life, nothing stood in the way of personal delight.

He wrote:

> I am deeply convinced that the Christian leader of the future is called to be completely irrelevant and to stand in this world with nothing to offer but his or her own vulnerable self....
>
> [This new kind of leader would have] an ardent desire to dwell in God's presence, to listen to God's voice, to look at God's beauty, to touch God's incarnate Word, and to taste fully God's infinite goodness.[11]

This brings us to the second change Nouwen argued that leaders need to make.

## From the Spectacular to the Ordinary

The temptation to be spectacular is ever present, and it will grab us by the throat when we least expect it. I read on the Internet last evening that people were scrambling to get tickets to hear a well-known pastor speak. I was surprised to be thinking, *No one scrambles for tickets to hear me speak. When am I ever going to get over this fading hope that I'm going to "make it"?* Then I shook off the uncontrolled rush of self-pity and pulled myself back together.

Fame and popularity are fun. Like a roller-coaster ride, they give us a rush. But we can't live on adrenaline, nor is God calling us to live in the limelight. While it might sound tempting to be able to turn stones into bread, true delight comes from allowing God to provide the bread and from being what he has called us to be. Real delight is in the ordinary work of life. Yes, we should do what we are gifted and called to do in the body of Christ, but our life is not just our work as ministers and leaders. We find the deepest level of satisfaction in ordinary service to others.

The ordinary is the milieu in which we live. We take out the garbage, get our car fixed, clean up the kitchen, shine our shoes, yield the right-of-way to the driver who doesn't see us and try not to call that person an unkind name. We sit at the table when our children come over for dinner, and we attempt to be a positive influence in their lives. We wonder how we have done as a parent, what our children say, how they conduct themselves, how they treat their spouses, how they instruct or discipline their children. Sometimes what we realize makes us feel sad, and sometimes we are filled with joy.

The truth is that, while it is great to be well known, it is much better to be loved. To be loved is tangible and concrete. We know we are loved when the children next door insist on hanging out with us in the yard, or when our golfing buddies just like being with us, no strings attached, or when the folks we hang out with at the coffee shop share their lives, opinions, faults, and burdens with us. A happy leader is based in a happy person. These are the ordinary parts of life, and who we are in the ordinary moments reveals whether Christ is the real thing in us. And that is the spectacular part of the disciple's life. We establish little beachheads for God where we can and ask him to use them.

The third change that Nouwen described is the change from being tempted to lead to allowing yourself to be led.

## From Leading to Being Led

Power will always be a temptation for leaders. Nouwen said it well: "The long painful history of the church is the history of people ever and again tempted to choose power over love, control over the cross, being a leader over being led."[12]

Leadership is actually about love, the cross, and being led. It is action taken for the benefit of another person. Good leaders do not control people; we serve and inspire them. The best leaders are also the best followers. They have learned submission, vulnerability, humility, and the power of fitting into a community. The greatest Christian leaders are those whose primary focus is following Christ. As Paul mentioned several times in one way or another, "Follow my example, as I follow the example of Christ."[13] Paul led with confidence. He wrote:

> We put no confidence in human effort, though I could have confidence in my own effort if anyone could.... I once thought these things were valuable, but now I consider them worthless because of what Christ has done.... For his sake I have discarded everything else, counting it all as garbage, so that I could gain Christ.[14]

Paul released control. He did not, however, become passive with regard to his efforts to reach the goal.

When Christian leaders relinquish control to God, it leads to happiness, because God determines the outcomes of our work as well as the level of recognition. There is great freedom in not trying to orchestrate how people respond to our actions. You have likely seen people bowling and how they contort, lean, and twist their body after they have released the ball. They may even yell at the ball as it drops into the gutter, as though all that noise and motion can determine results. Once the ball has left the bowler's hand, there is nothing left to do. Once you release your actions and have done your best, then live freely, knowing that God alone will determine results.

Nouwen spoke of this new direction:

> The way of the Christian leader is not the way of upward mobility in which our world has invested so much, but the way of downward mobility ending on the cross. This might sound morbid and masochistic, but for those who have heard his voice of the first love and said yes to it, the downward-moving way of Jesus is the way to the joy and the peace of God, a joy and peace that is not of this world.[15]

This new way of life is determined by being able to hear God's voice. Only the sound of God's voice can satisfy the human need for affirmation and direction.

Some leaders make it sound as if God speaks to them a lot. I really don't know about that, but I know that for me to hear God's voice, I must be in a position to listen. God's voice often seems hidden, and when he does speak it can be softly. This means I must be quiet, alone, and reading Scripture. Every once in a while I need to spend extended time alone with God. Without that, I regress to using my skills to get people to do what I want them to do.

I have had only one dream in my life that I remember vividly. In the dream I was involved in a process of discernment with some wise people. The discussion centered on my calling. A woman who seemed to be in charge walked up behind me. She leaned down and cupped her hands over my ear and whispered, "You have been chosen, anointed a teacher to the nations."

The interesting point was that the anointing was not to be based in an institution. I took this to mean that my influence would be more organic, detached from the mainstream organizational model. The group continued to talk, but the woman cut off the discussion and dismissed everyone. She casually turned to speak with another person while I was left wondering what it all meant.

I had been seeking direction from God for some time regarding what size of an organization I should build. Should I raise funds and hire staff and approach the challenge organizationally? I decided to take the dream as a word from God and not to build an organization. This was not easy for me, because I have built and led organizations; I know how to do that. The harder course for me was to wait for people to invite me to speak. So I took the advice of the ancient sage who said, "Seek not to speak, seek to have something to say." I wrote down my thoughts and waited.

For the last ten years I have traveled the world teaching, writing books, and reaching leaders via the written and spoken word with curricula and videos. Many I have trained and worked with have developed large organizations and are now carrying the message forward. I needed to hear from God about my future, and I did. I don't believe, however, that I would have heard much if I hadn't cultivated a listening ear through the spiritual exercises of my covenant community.

Not long ago I walked through a house in London set back just off City Road. It is the John Wesley House, a small rectory attached to a historic Methodist church. Wesley lived and worked from this home, which looks as if it was built for hobbits. Wesley was only five feet two, and the house seemed to fit. After logging over 250,000 miles on horseback as a traveling preacher, he spent the last ten years of his life preaching, writing, and doing pastoral work. His last words were, "And best of all, God is with us." A statue of Wesley stands in front of the church and house. The words inscribed on its front are the antithesis of Shakespeare's words from *The Merry Wives of Windsor*, "The world is my oyster." It says, "The world is my parish."

What makes Christian leaders happy? It is when the world is no longer our oyster to consume, but our parish to serve.

# Making a Dent in the World

## REHABILITATE YOUR IDEA OF HOW YOU MAKE YOUR MARK

Do nothing out of selfish ambition or vain conceit.

**Philippians 2:3**

I want them ... to feel my power.

**Sir Winston Churchill**

**IT IS CURRENTLY** fashionable to say, "Make a dent in the universe."[1] However, I can't think of anything more confusing to a leader than to know how to do that. Second in degree of difficulty is connecting one's effort to results. Is a leader required to be exhausted at all times? One of the late Steve Jobs's primary characteristics was exhaustion; his creative entourage also seemed to sleep little. Is that what is required to make a dent in the world? Is working day and night the only way to be a powerful person?

The apostle Paul worked hard to present every disciple mature in Christ. He considered himself a steward, presenting his work to God. He worked hard but in sync with God: "I strenuously contend with all the energy Christ so powerfully works in me."[2] Paul considered his work challenging: "My dear children, for whom I am again in the pains of childbirth until Christ is formed in you!"[3] However, what made his work difficult was not the hours, but its nature. Leadership is emotionally exhausting; the heart takes a beating. Recently a judge working in leadership in his church told me, "None of this stuff is very hard until you add real people to the mix. It was so easy when we had only the enthused, the faithful, and the hungry few gathered around us. Now as we stretch to reach a larger circle — people who are a little less enthused, a little less faithful, a little less hungry — it is more challenging."[4] I couldn't agree more.

Everyone makes an impression, regardless of their intention. At times the impression we make is the opposite of the one we want to make. For instance, a man on a job interview tries to be the person the company wants to hire and goes overboard. It is obvious to the interviewer that the résumé is padded and the applicant is trying too hard. Instead of leaving the impression of competence, the man leaves one of dishonesty and desperation. Better for him to have not worked at making an impression, but to have allowed who he is to create an impression.

Think of it this way. If you have shaken hands with a bricklayer, you may have winced from the power of the grip. Bricklayers' strong hands are a by-product of the work they do. They don't start out to have strong hands; it comes with the profession. Similarly, leaders aren't strong because we are trying to be strong; we are strong because of other inherent characteristics, such as kindness, patience, perseverance, self-control, great faith, and courage. Scripture wants us to be others-centered and warns against trying to impress others with our talents.[5]

In this chapter we will survey the lives of several leaders who left a distinct impression on the world — a historian, a philosopher, a politician, and a public intellectual — with an eye for what we might learn from them about how to lead more like Christ.

## Josephus: A Selfish Man Driven to Make a Dent

Josephus was a significant historian of the first century. He was a man who sought to have an impact on others. Born seven years after the resurrection, Josephus grew up in a world in which Peter led the church and Paul was traveling throughout the Mediterranean starting churches. Josephus was producing thick books of history during the time when the Gospels were being written. He lived the first half of his life in Palestine and the second half in Rome.

Josephus was religious as a young man. He even studied for three years under a hermit named Bannus. After this study, he decided to become a Pharisee. He was young, bright, and ambitious. At age twenty-six, he was asked to represent the Jewish leadership in Rome when a number of Jewish priests had been arrested. He negotiated the release of the priests, and this enhanced his power. While he was negotiating in Rome, Paul was there under house arrest. Josephus was known to have influence with Nero's wife Sabina, who helped in the negotiations. This was, of course, no help to Paul, who was executed on Nero's order.

Upon his return to Palestine, Josephus was asked to raise an army to resist the Romans under General Vespasian. He managed to raise an army of one hundred thousand men. Vespasian's army proved to be too much, however, and it surrounded Josephus's men in the city of Jotapata. It was a small, walled city and after forty-seven days the Romans penetrated the walls and killed forty thousand citizens. Toward the end of the battle, Josephus did something that turned him from hero to villain in a single day.[6] He jumped into a pit to escape and found that it was connected to a tunnel and cave where forty upper-class citizens of the town were hiding with food and water.

After the battle, Vespasian was searching bodies, looking for the famous and charismatic star of the Jewish people. Josephus left the cave but three days later was captured and promised safe passage if the forty people would come out. The citizens in the cave would have none of it. They felt it would be a total dishonor and insisted on committing suicide. Josephus was authorized to return to the cave to present an impassioned plea to them against suicide, but they were not moved. They drew lots and the agreement was to slit each other's throats one by one until the last man slit his own. Josephus somehow managed to get the last lot and when it came down to it, he and the other remaining man decided enough had died and they gave themselves up. Word got out about what he had done and Josephus was hated by the Jews from that time forward. Vespasian kept Josephus a prisoner for two years. He presented himself as a prophet and predicted that Vespasian would become emperor of Rome, and indeed he did. Vespasian gradually accepted

Josephus's self-description, released him from prison, and brought him to Jerusalem. He asked Josephus to plead with his fellow Jews to keep the temple safe by surrendering. Josephus's biographer, Geoffrey Williamson, described the process.

> He had time and time again ridden round beleaguered Jerusalem in dangerous proximity to the walls, explaining to the deluded defenders the hopelessness of further resistance, and pleading with them while the tears ran down his face to yield to the merciful Roman whose one desire was to end their agony.[7]

The Jews weren't buying it. One account says they hit him with a rock and knocked him out. The complete destruction of Jerusalem followed; the city and the temple were leveled.

Josephus lived out the last thirty years of his life with a comfortable stipend in an imperial palace in Rome where he spent his time writing. He wrote the *History of the Jewish War.* There was an underlying theme to his work that the Jews needed to give up being Jewish. He had become a propagandist for Rome. Josephus was the consummate opportunist. He thought of his own life and welfare as the ultimate good. He left a mark, all right. It is one of selfishness and empty conceit.[8]

As I read about the life of Josephus, I thought back through my life and wondered, *When as a leader have I left people behind for personal gain?* What can Christian leaders learn from the life of Josephus?

**Not to abandon people who have trusted us.** Josephus turned on his own people, both in the siege of Jotapata and later when he represented Roman interests during the siege of Jerusalem. In both cases, he was duplicitous. He proved not to be a trustworthy man.

Whenever people take a promotion, they leave fellow workers, congregations, or groups and societies behind. To be fair, in almost every circumstance the group replaces them. Whether they are simply leaving or are indeed abandoning people has to do with the condition of the people they leave and the motives for moving on. A person has a sense of his or her true motives, an inner knowledge. The saving grace is being honest with ourselves and others. Even if the people around us are kind and understanding, leaders can't use that as an out. We must struggle with this issue and hear from God.

For Christian leaders, knowing our motivation means seeking God in prayer and hearing from him at a deep level. When we hear God's voice and do his will, Christlikeness is built in us. The more we listen and hear from God, the more Christlike our character becomes. Hearing and obeying God's voice becomes a way of life and our hearts are nourished by this closeness.

*To do nothing out of selfishness and rivalry.* Philippians 2:3 says, "Do nothing out of selfish ambition or vain conceit. Rather, in humility value others above yourselves." The point of the verse is that whatever you do to have an impact on the world, don't let it be birthed in rivalry with others or in a misguided overconfidence. Those who try to orchestrate their influence always make a different one than God intended for them to make.[9] This was certainly true for Josephus.

Most Christian leaders are not as blatantly selfish as Josephus. However, many claim, "I want to make God famous" or "I want to reach my community," but their true motive is advancing their career or their power. I find that many would-be consultants are getting younger and younger. They want to be a resource person within their favorite realm. They want to speak, write, teach, and charge generous fees that could create a pleasurable career for them. The hitch in this plan is that before you can become a consultant, you must first accomplish something. People hire consultants because of their wisdom, which, of course, is based on experience.

Rivalry is subtle, but competition is a natural part of life; most pastors and other Christian leaders can't help but sense they are in competition with other churches for members or with other mission organizations for donor dollars. It affects a leader's job and livelihood when other churches attract his or her members and giving goes down. There are just so many dollars allotted for continuing education in church budgets. Who will get those dollars? It will go to those who can grow, hire staff, pay their bills, and continue as an organization. I do not believe the marketplace is evil and it often sorts out what is a quality product from what is inferior. But make no mistake about it, in the marketplace it is the survival of the fittest. One only needs to read the history of the competition between Steve Jobs and Bill Gates to prove the point.

And so leaders are told to create a "brand" so that they can gain more readers, larger audiences or congregations, and more Twitter followers and Facebook friends. A brand might be an artistic look or some other avant-garde expression, or it might be an emphasis for which you want to be known. I read about a young pastor who was described as one who put the "hip" back into discipleship. I have to admit that this is a catchy line; I felt a twinge of envy when I read it since I thought that was me. But then I discovered that my "hip" was more like an artificial hip to the younger generation. Even though I am on Medicare, I am much more drawn to the new than I am to the old. I like new gadgets, new books, new films, new clothes, new cars, and new ideas. I would loathe to be considered out of touch or irrelevant. This is a dangerous part of my personality and I must be careful that I don't do things simply because I don't want to be left behind (and I am not talking about the book series by that name!). Leaders can fall in love with subtle new ideas that slowly move us away from our core beliefs. We start to compromise on the need to evangelize the world and to take a stand on moral issues; before we realize it, our core convictions have been hollowed out by modernity.

We're also told we need to be "on the leading edge." A few years ago it was hip to remove all religious symbols from church buildings. The cross in particular was to be visually subtle, not front and center. The idea was to make the building more welcoming to unbelievers. How powerful the drive for relevancy can be! The rage was to extract all the traditional symbols and practices so that you could reach scores of new people. The fallacy of it was that non-Christians are not commanded to go to church; furthermore, they have no plans to attend church. They are not thinking about the order of service or look. There were some fast-growing churches that did extract these symbols and went avant-garde, but it was the talent of the preachers more than anything else. And that this trend passed out of vogue in ten years is instructive. So don't be so easily impressed by apparent success.

But what is a leader to do? How can we do this work of leading and not be competitive? The bottom line is that we can't. Drive is essential if anything is to be accomplished. God has made us competitive beings. To deny this fact shows an alarming misunderstanding of how humans are designed. Some people are better at building churches, singing, or writing a book than others. Ambition is essential if we are going to obey Christ and fulfill the Great Commission. It is a matter of channeling our competitiveness for the purpose of Christ. A good example of this in action is that of a philosopher at the University of Southern California, the late Dallas Willard.

## Dallas Willard: A Humble Man Committed to Not Try to Make Things Happen

For several years I was a member of a group that included the philosopher and writer Dallas Willard. In one of our daily sessions he commented, "A number of years ago I made a commitment to not try to make anything happen." This statement is mysterious. It could be attributed to his being a philosopher who liked to leave his hearers scratching their heads. Another explanation could be that he was a bit detached, living in an ivory tower if you will, and not in the dirt and grime of real life with the rest of us. Or perhaps this was just an unrealistic statement by a highly gifted person who had many beating a path to his door, a man who seemed passive but in fact was not.

It turned out that these words expressed the conviction of a man who was impressed by God to make the commitment. Their context was a speech he was asked to give. As Dallas sat on the platform, he decided that he would not try to make an impression. He wouldn't try to move people with emotional flair; he wouldn't attempt to wow them with eloquence or with deep philosophical ponderings they couldn't understand, with a seeming obtuseness they would blame on themselves.[10]

I asked Dallas what he meant and even challenged his premise. "When you write a lecture, you are making something happen," I countered. "The same when you write a book." He answered, "No, my commitment is to not attempt to create interest in my work. My commitment is to do good work, and then people can choose. God either will bless it or he won't, but what happens to my efforts is not my concern."

Consequently, he wrote books without having a publisher because he wanted the freedom to work on something as long as he needed to, without deadlines. It was the reason he didn't know his book sales, nor did he sell his books at speaking engagements. He didn't even have a speaking fee! What do you do with a man like this? Admire him? To admire Dallas costs us nothing; to follow his example could be traumatic, for it would rip control of our lives out of our hands.

Dallas provided us with a modern-day example of what Jesus did and what Paul taught. Jesus continually warned his disciples and the people he healed not to spread the word about his miracles. It would have made him prematurely famous and would have disrupted God's plan for the world. At the wedding at Cana he even tried to hold off his mother's request that he turn water into wine: "'Woman, why do you involve me?' Jesus replied. 'My hour has not yet come.'"[11] I think most of us would have jumped at the chance to be the center of attention and to advance our careers. There was no guile in Jesus' soul. He competed against the Enemy, the one who darkens the mind and soils the soul. Jesus was not conceited. In fact, he was the very opposite: humble.

Conceit, or thinking of oneself more than one should, is the currency of contemporary culture and power. It pervades every realm of life. From automobile ads to health-care products, we see promoted the belief that, compared to others, we are the best or among the best. Many public figures have the Mussolini look, taken from that famous film clip of the Italian dictator in his military uniform. His arms are folded, his jaw juts out, and he has a look on his face that says, "I'm the best, il Duce — the leader; I am a gift to the Italian people." Mussolini could strut sitting down. I think we all know the type. It doesn't matter if they are an Italian fascist or the secretary or treasurer of a church — people who are full of arrogance are easy to spot.

Dallas had a great deal of influence among thoughtful leaders and readers. He made serious headway in recapturing what it means to be a follower of Christ and what is the very nature of the gospel. In some ways, he was a modern Martin Luther. He brought a reformation to the definition of the words *faith*, *grace*, *belief*, *commitment*, and *kingdom*. What the next generation believes about the gospel has been shaped in part by this avuncular philosopher; yet it was never his goal to have such power.

This leads us into a discussion of power.

# The Nature of Power

Power is the effect one person has on another.

## No One Knows How Much Power They Have

In his book *Culture Making*, Andy Crouch made the point that money, sex, and power represent the basic temptations and power bases of life. While the first two are measurable — you can count your money and you know when you are having sex — not so with power.

We can feel the difference in power when people call us because they need our help, and when we call others because we need their help. Being interviewed for a job is a much different feeling than being the interviewer. I have spent much of my life raising funds and have observed these differences in power. When I called someone early in our relationship or had no relationship with that person and was essentially cold-calling, I was at his mercy. He had all the power. Once the relationship was established and I had built some trust, then my phone calls and emails were returned, because trust and respect had developed. It's different when a person of great power asks a potential donor for funds. In that scenario, the donor feels honored and may actually compete with others to give, because the donor senses that a donation will enhance their career or will be good public relations for what they do.

As I gained confidence as a fundraiser, it became a joy to

interact with those who gave to our cause. I do recall, however, that on more than one occasion I became frustrated with the process. I knew a donor who wanted to sponsor an event for me. The donor paid for the event and offered to help me with a future project. I thought we had a growing and productive relationship because we had mutual interests. I called later to present the needs of another project but he wouldn't return my call. I kept after him for a few more days, and finally his assistant told me he was not interested and couldn't speak with me. I sent off an angry letter to the donor, excoriating him for failing to show me respect. I went on to accuse him of being hypocritical because he would never treat Billy Graham the way he was treating me. I am sure I was right about that, but then again, I am not Billy Graham. I was angry that I didn't have the power I thought I had, and that made me feel humiliated. My conceit violated the theme of this chapter and I was thinking more of myself than a humble servant of Christ would have reason to do.[12] I had grown accustomed to my power and I didn't like it when it was gone.

## No One Ever Has Enough Power

Ironically, the most powerful person in the world, the president of the United States, doesn't have enough power. He doesn't have enough power to feed the world's hungry, eradicate poverty, end wars and genocide, or even solve America's financial problems. He does have great power, though, and he can use it every day for good. The early church, which spread from Jerusalem throughout the Middle East, Asia Minor, and Europe, didn't entirely change the world, but it did change it substantially.[13] So while Christians never have enough power, we do have plenty of power. Paul wrote in Romans 1:16, "I am not ashamed of the gospel, because it is the power of God that brings salvation to everyone who believes: first to the Jew, then to the Gentile." There is enough power to do what

71

God values the most—saving "everyone who believes." We don't have the power to force belief, we don't have the power to change people, and we cannot control people once they do become followers of Christ. But we do have the power to spread this message by life and words.

# Winston Churchill: An Imperfect Man Who Used His Power for Others

When a person of power has an institution, a nation, or military might behind him, it multiplies that person's power. This was certainly true of Winston Churchill. He had some power as a member of the British Parliament and the cultural elite. His ability to give a good speech and write an excellent book gave him power. Between 1930 and 1940, he was in disfavor, the decade known now as his wilderness years. He spent most of the time in his Elizabethan-era home at Chartwell, a three-hundred-acre estate twenty-five miles from Parliament. There he painted, wrote some of his best works, and famously built a stone wall. He also agonized over being out of power and even plotted to force his way back in. Most thought he would never rise to power again since he already was over sixty years old.

Churchill was in many ways an egomaniac, consumed with power and sure that he was born to do great things. This was a belief his mother shared. She helped him to create a heroic story of escape as a prisoner of war during the Second Boer War. It wasn't that it didn't happen; it was that it was publicized and dramatized for his benefit, which helped him get elected to Parliament. After the First World War, Churchill wrote a long book about the war and all it meant to England and Europe. One of his critics, A. J. Balfour, said of Churchill's book, "Winston has written an enormous book about himself and called it *The World Crisis*."[14]

Churchill was once asked a question by a young socialite about the nature of man. He responded, "We are all worms. But I really think I am a glow worm."[15] He believed he was special, that he was called to do great things. When he was named prime minister in 1940, he relished it; for this he was born.

The historian Paul Johnson asked, "How did one man do so much, for so long, and so effectively?"[16] Churchill was a prolific writer; he spent much of his life turning words into cash to pay his bills. He published more than ten million words, more than most professional writers. It is obvious that he was ambitious; in fact he had enough ambition for a thousand men. He always aimed high. He worked hard, even though he did much of it from his bed in the mornings and he slept very little. He worked diligently to make himself a master orator. He had talent, but it was nothing without hard work. I think Churchill's ambition is summed up by a statement he made as prime minister. He was once seen walking up and down in an empty cabinet room after a major sacking, saying aloud, "I want them ... to feel my power."[17]

What kind of impression was Churchill trying to make? While he was clearly advancing his career, he also used power on behalf of others. He was an imperfect man who took his own bathtub to war and who loved all the advantages of wealth and power. But in the end, he is considered by many to be the most courageous and determined leader of the twentieth century. He used his power to make a dent in the world. Winston Churchill was not a Christian leader. However, he saved Western civilization with his great courage in standing alone against Hitler in the early years of World War II.

Churchill is a good example of a person who used his inner strength to serve the greater good and to not compromise liberty and freedom to avoid great sacrifice. Hitler thought Churchill would sue for peace and submit, but he wouldn't. His beliefs would not allow him to compromise. History has dubbed him "the Last

Lion." There is much to admire about him. Some may not easily see Christ in that five-feet-six-inch chubby curmudgeon, but when it comes to leading others into a sacrificial mission for a great moral cause, he is at the top of the heap.

Power is woven into the fabric of human personality and is impossible to unravel. In fact, we all know that "their work will be shown for what it is, because the Day will bring it to light. It will be revealed with fire, and the fire will test the quality of each person's work."[18] God alone can sort out motivation, and then we will know. Until then, Christians are called to use power for good.

## How Can Christians Use Power for Good?

Christians are called to use their power to impress Christ on those around us. But I want to be careful not to hang the millstone of "changing the world" around your neck. Yes, we are responsible to make an impact where we live, work, and play. But that is quite different from changing the world.

Andy Crouch defined cultural power as "the ability to successfully propose a new cultural good."[19] A cultural good is something concrete, a tangible artifact, whether a book, a tool, or a building. But an artifact is more than a fork found in an archaeological dig. It can also be a mass-produced, inexpensive object that reflects the contemporary culture, such as a mobile phone. The mobile phone has affected how we do business, relate to others, pay our bills, drive our cars, manage our families, and even how we decide where we will live. As Christian leaders, we must recognize that many of those things we hold sacred — modes of evangelism, preaching styles, Christian music, even the gospel itself — are cultural artifacts. All reflect the consumer culture in which we live. There is one thing more serious than the gospel being a cultural artifact; it is that a poorly behaved, nominal Christian is a cultural artifact—common, and a product of our culture.

Christians have always found it difficult to speak of their own power. We talk about God's power working through us, which is essential for any work that is to be done in his name. No doubt the early church attracted new followers through miracles and acts of power. This is the dominant theme in the first half of the book of Acts. Virtually every major address given in Acts was a result of a miracle or a conflict that was created by miracles. It is a shame how the church via the media has cheapened "signs and wonders." The general perception is that miracles are the private property of the carnival that is Christian television.

However, a different kind of power that can be used for good is personal power. Any person who is recognized for their achievements has personal power. For example, judges who are followers of Christ have power in a community. Their character is crucial to the integrity of their work, but when they decide in their nonjudicial life to speak for Christ, they likely have more influence with colleagues than they would if they were, for example, plumbers.

Even though there is deep suspicion in churches regarding power, Christians are called to be stewards of power. In fact, this is a crucial piece of God's plan for reaching our world. We are to use our personal power to influence those around us in our everyday lives. This is why Christian athletes are important to those they influence. The youth of a community or nation are deeply impressed by the famous. Few people are as recognizable as athletes. When athletes are willing to use their platform for Christ, it makes a difference.

But a Christian doesn't have to be famous to influence others for Christ. A coffee shop owner has the power to create an environment, sponsor events, and employ certain kinds of people in a way that influences the community for Christ. The stay-at-home mom with schoolchildren can have ongoing influence among the families that are connected to the schools and her children's athletic teams. We should make it a matter of ongoing prayer and effort to learn how to leverage our power to help people find the Christ who will transform them, and to make a dent in the world.

## Congruent with How God Made You

I return here to the subject found in the second sentence of this chapter: "I can't think of anything more confusing to a leader than how to [make a dent in the world]." There seems to be confusion about how hard a leader ought to work, how much a leader should plan, and how thoroughly a leader should strategize. The answer is to learn about yourself and work in a way congruent with how God made you.

Jesus was the perfect balance of a person who served others from his character. He was not selfish, nor was he selfless. Jesus had a drive to please his Father. He had ideas that challenged the authorities, and he had plans that he inspired his followers to execute. His power to make a dent in the world was in his person. Make no mistake about it, being God is an advantage. Jesus could read the heart of every person. He didn't trust people because he knew human nature.[20] Jesus was not passive; he wasn't just following his nose. He didn't wake up like a goose to a new world every day; he had a strategy. When Jesus spoke to Nicodemus, confronted the corruption in the temple, and spoke with the woman at the well, he was acting out of his personal character. He was being himself, and it inspired his followers. They remembered his words and actions and, as Scripture says, "believed" in him.[21]

Eugene Peterson is a modern-day example of someone who acts in a way that is congruent with how God made him; consequently, he has made a significant dent in the world.

# Eugene Peterson:
# Doing It His Own Way

The leadership conference known as Catalyst presented seventy-nine-year-old Eugene Peterson with its Lifetime Achievement Award. There is some irony in this since Peterson is the antithesis of a good bit of American evangelicalism. He is known for castigating the church for being too achievement-oriented and locked in on measurable results. He is famous for saying that the church has never been successful; we have slogged along for two thousand years and this is not likely to change. Catalyst is considered cutting-edge and hip; Peterson is neither. He has criticized many of the leadership models that are presented to pastors. He has stated that almost all of them are the CEO, activist, "get things done" type.

So for what achievement was he rewarded? Peterson pastored the same church for over thirty years, and it never exceeded five hundred attendees — less than 25 percent of one's definition of a megachurch. He wasn't being rewarded for his great preaching — you have to strain to hear his voice, and he barely moves his arms, modulates his voice, or moves his body in any noticeable way. He rarely tells a story or cracks a joke. He is very serious. The typical distracted, superficial, contemporary mind cannot tolerate his presentations. I can't think of any real methodological innovation that he pioneered, curriculum he wrote, or special outreach ministry that he developed.

Peterson tells a story of being the keynote speaker at a conference (not Catalyst) that represented everything he is not. He returned home and felt that all the God in him had been sucked out. Being a scholar, he spent several days reading Karl Barth's works on systematic theology. Barth took him back to his true beliefs. When we hear this we are tempted to throw up our hands and admit, "There is no hope for me. I don't even *own* a book by

Karl Barth." That may be true, but what we do have is a pathway back home to our core beliefs. Peterson admits that the conference's ways and means were not for him. The Catalyst conference leaders wanted to have beliefs more like Peterson's. Peterson was given this award because they believed he was right and they aspired to have their beliefs be more like his. They were acknowledging that he represents the best of Christian leadership.

The only reason we know anything about Peterson is his books. His actual results are more in his character and in his pen than in the numbers he has created. Peterson's life says that we can find our own way as leaders, and when we do it for the right reasons, the best of us comes out. In Peterson's case, "the best in him" was his background in languages and his love of literature, philosophy, and the arts, which produced a series of marvelous writings that helped shape a generation of leaders who desperately needed what he had to say. For that, the pastors of America wanted to say, "Thank you, and we thank God for you. Thank you for your stubbornness, for your commitment to the pastoral life, and for restoring the historic meaning to the calling."

I know the feeling that comes upon us as we admire Peterson. We want to honor him but we can't understand how we could ever be like him. He, like Dallas Willard, never set out to make an impression or control what people thought of him, yet he has accomplished much and become well known. I don't think he is impressed by his fame or thinks it is good for him or any other pastor.

Peterson is unique. He was a language whiz in seminary and enrolled in Johns Hopkins University to earn a PhD in Semitic languages. But he discovered that unless all he was learning was lived, it was useless. He became a pastor and was asked to start his own church in Baltimore. He was able to lead the church into a building program; later, attendance declined 30 percent. He went to his supervisor for advice. His counsel was for Peterson to start another building program — something concrete that was not as ethereal as the spiritual life. Peterson didn't know what to do, but he was sure he would not start another building program.

He claimed he didn't know how to pastor, but he also didn't believe in copying other pastors. He started meeting with local pastors on Tuesdays, and they joined together to learn how to pastor. He was committed to ministry that was local, personal, and patient. He saw that his job was prayer, listening, silence, worship, "being there," and the exposition of Scripture. He went through a six-year funk, a "dark night of the soul" experience. During this time he went to his board and resigned; he claimed he didn't know how to pastor, mainly because he had to run the church. His board told him, "We will run the church; you figure out how to pastor." When he emerged, he began to write to pastors. *Five Smooth Stones for Pastoral Work*, *A Long Obedience in the Same Direction*, *Working the Angles* — all are groundbreaking books in the face of the American pastoral experience.

One of my favorite Peterson books is *Subversive Spirituality*, a collection of essays that would shake even the most confident of secular leaders. Peterson calls for all pastors to strive to be irrelevant and unnecessary. He considers a pastor's job to be modest in nature and mundane in execution. Pastors are not important to the secular community, but in the kingdom of God, they are crucial. They are to pay attention to what God is doing and point it out to their congregations. For over thirty years, Peterson labored as pastor of Christ the King Church. During his pastoral years he started to translate Scripture for his church members so they could better grasp the meaning of the words. Over time, this led to the creation of the Bible paraphrase called *The Message*. It could be said that listening to Peterson talk about life, literature, and leading is a celestial feast.

## What Is to Be Learned?

In this chapter we have surveyed men of impact: a historian, a philosopher, a politician, and a pastor. What is to be learned? Each had his own kind of power. Only one, the historian, used it for ill. Willard and Peterson were devout. The source of their impact is obvious; each could say along with Paul, "Follow my example, as I follow the example of Christ."[22] What I find most inviting about Willard and Peterson is that they did not seek power — they were given it. Unlike Churchill, neither one of these men said, "I want them to feel all my power."

I do nevertheless believe there are places in Christian leadership for people like Churchill. They are leaders who sense their destiny and are just the right person to change history. Sometimes Christian leaders fail and have bad motives, but if their work is for the kingdom of God, then it is all worth it. Whatever power God gives a leader with which to make an impact, it is a gift to be used. Use it with care.

# The Leader's Worldview

## REHABILITATE YOUR INTERPRETATION OF THE WORLD

In your relationships with one another, have the same mindset as Christ Jesus: Who, being in very nature God, did not consider equality with God something to be used to his own advantage.

**Philippians 2:5 – 6**

They are not of the world, even as I am not of it.

**John 17:16**

We live at the mercy of our ideas.

**Dallas Willard**

SOME RESEARCH indicates that a person's worldview is determined by age thirteen.[1] Mine was pretty much in place when I was fourteen and my newspaper manager came to our house to fire me. I was no profile in courage; I had been sloppy on my route and had received too many complaints. My primary transgression was spending my collection money before I paid my bill to the newspaper manager. There I sat with my mother, my paper manager, and my sister. My mother was humiliated, my manager was disappointed, and my sister was delighted that I had finally been caught at something. I usually laughed out loud when called before authorities. I didn't that day, but I still had a smirk on my face. Exasperated with my demeanor, the manager yelled at me, "Bill, what are you going to do with yourself?" I lived on the brink of disaster. I was failing in school, I was academically ineligible for freshman basketball, and I was hanging out with some questionable characters. Earlier that year I had been kicked out of school for cutting lunch, and I had also run away from home for a night.

My answer to his question was all the more audacious in light of the context. "My plan," I said confidently, "is to attend college on a basketball scholarship." Then it was his turn to smirk. Only four out of every one hundred thousand boys who play high school basketball play college basketball on a scholarship, and I was not even on the freshman squad at my school. But I knew something my newspaper manager didn't. Even though I was ineligible to play basketball, I practiced at least one hour a day, no matter what, and I was good — better than the players on the freshman team.

I would summarize my worldview as follows:

1. You must do it yourself; don't count on others.

2. If you want something, you can get it if you outwork everyone, even those who may be smarter or more gifted than you.

3. If I don't get a basketball scholarship, I will not be able to attend college, and I will need to get a job or join the army.

4. Religion is too restrictive. I want to enjoy life, and Christians don't have any fun.

My view of the world and how it worked was shaped by my upbringing. My mother, sister, and I lived with my grandparents because my father left us (or was run off, depending on whom you talk to). I never met him. My mother was hardworking, very loving, and went out on dates, despite my grandparents' disapproval. Her take-home pay was thirty-nine dollars a week. The first twelve years of my life we attended a Holiness church in Indianapolis, Indiana. I reacted so strongly to the legalism and drab lifestyle that I didn't attend another church service until I was twenty-one. And then only because of a beautiful girl.

It was when I started playing on a team that I first knew I was different. I would look around at basketball practice or at games and see fathers of the other players. My mother came to see me play a few times when she could get a ride with her boyfriend. But after he was seriously injured in an automobile accident, she was not able to attend any more games. I played four years of college basketball and three years for Athletes in Action, and my mother never saw me play. This reinforced my belief that my life was mine to make. I was on my own.

This part of my worldview still explains some of my behavior today. Rather than compete in the crowd, I prefer to go away by myself and compete on my own terms. I am more comfortable doing things on my own than depending on others. The value of hard work, discipline, and a clear goal is deeply engrained in me, along with the idea that if I want something done I must do it myself. My significant life decisions were run through this filter. Consequently, I chose a writing career over a more conventional academic life because I wanted to control what I studied. Whenever I wanted to break out of an institutional model, I created a new ministry. I have always enjoyed the freedom of launching out into the deep, creating the funding, and leading the charge. Even my decision thirteen years ago to spend the rest of my life writing and teaching was rooted in my worldview.

## Assimilating My Worldview with New Life in Christ

I was not religious, but the Christian message attracted me because I was interested in meaning. I accepted a basketball scholarship to Oral Roberts University partly because of a friend of mine who had preceded me to ORU. He was a changed man and I knew why — religion. He was the biggest hell-raiser I knew, and I was stunned that he had taken the plunge. At the time, I was trying to make sense of my life and thought that I might be able to figure things out if I went to a Christian college. However, if I were to attend a Christian school, it would need to have a really good basketball team. The college and students at ORU impressed me favorably, and I came to the critical decision, "I think I could become one of them."

Before I came to Christ, my worldview was centered on accomplishing my goals and making my life work. Now I was coming up against a worldview that said I needed to live by faith and give my dreams and goals to God. I kept hearing phrases like, "We can't do anything on our own" and "Lord, I did nothing; it was all your doing." Christians seemed to look down on good works, almost as though they were some lower form of existence.

This confused me. The worldview of the Christians around me seemed quite different from my own. Suddenly I was up against a theology of passivity. How could I blend my worldview of the need for hard work and discipline with a life of faith, grace, submission, and sacrifice? How would I get anything accomplished in such an environment? If I knew anything, it was that I had worked my way out of being a docile loser into a confident winner. When I saw a problem, I figured out a way to solve it. To make things worse, I was a good salesman; I knew how to get people to do things. I started to reflect on what made Jesus such an effective leader and on what I could learn from him about what a Christian leader's worldview should be.

## A Worldview Rooted in Our Connection to the Father

Jesus famously said, "My kingdom is not of this world."[2] Some of the most chilling words in all of Scripture are found in the interchange between Pilate, Jesus, and the crowds. After Pilate found no fault with Jesus, he attempted to free him, but the crowds would have none of it; they cried out, "Crucify him! Crucify him!" Pilate finally was exasperated with Jesus and asked, "Where do you come from? ... Do you refuse to speak to me? ... Don't you realize I have power either to free you or to crucify you?" Jesus answered, "*You would have no power over me if it were not given to you from above.*"[3]

Jesus knew that everything that happened in this world was orchestrated from another world, and so he submitted his will to the Father in everything he did. Paul wrote that Jesus, "being in very nature God, did not consider equality with God something to be used to his own advantage."[4]

It seems obvious, doesn't it, that a significant lesson in Christian leadership is to turn your eyes heavenward and talk to your leader about what you should be doing. This world is not the source of God's kingdom, and to get God's kingdom or rule on earth, Christian leaders must begin in heaven. We are not to look inward at our own capacity but heavenward, to how God wants to use our abilities.

As the God-man, Jesus had perfect human capacity to accomplish everything he did in his own power, and yet he accomplished his mission by working in concert with the larger agenda found in the triune relationship. Jesus teaches us by example that our worldview needs to be rooted in our connection to the Father.

Jesus recognized that the hour had come for his death and resurrection, meaning that his mission on earth was almost complete. In the only detailed conversation we have between him and the Father he said, "And now, Father, glorify me in your presence with the glory I had with you before the world began."[5] The understanding that there is a place or state outside of time, where God dwelled before the earth or solar system existed, is essential to carrying out any sacrificial mission. Jesus wanted to return to this existence, and he wanted his followers to experience it as well. And according to the moral imperative set by God, he had to die in order for that to happen. He told his Father in the hearing of Peter, James, and John, "You granted him authority over all people that he [meaning himself] might give eternal life to all those you have given him. Now this is eternal life: that they know you, the only true God, and Jesus Christ, whom you have sent."[6]

Jesus later gave his disciples this authority in what is called the Great Commission.[7] He authorized them to do what he had already done — make disciples. When it comes down to the essence of our lives on this earth, it is to be disciples. And when it comes to the primary focus of our work, it is to make disciples. This is the only work that every Christ follower has been authorized to do. Jesus simply passed on to his followers the task that the Father had given to him.

At the end of the conversation, Jesus declared to his Father, *"I have brought you glory on earth by finishing the work you gave me to do."*[8] What could be more satisfying to the Christian leader than to please the Father and complete the work he has given you? Jesus' worldview was that success was accomplishing the mission God had given him to do. This worldview is the singular motivation of Christian leadership. Christian leadership is not primarily about technique; it is about why you are in leadership and your reasons for what you do. It is also about whom you are trying to please. Jesus had to be a leader to accomplish the mission that God had given him.

## My Journey in Pleasing the Father

Growing up, I had no earthly father to please. However, I was eager to please adult authority figures, especially men. I made a special connection with my high school basketball coach. He recognized both my talent and my problems. He came to my home and told my mother that he wanted me to go to a Fellowship of Christian Athletes conference in Henderson Harbor, New York. He believed in me and provided the funds for the trip.

My desire to please Coach Gene Ring drove me to practice hard. He was Catholic and religion played a significant role in his life. The Henderson Harbor experience didn't work on me because of my resistance to religion at that age. I reacted strongly against the legalism and customs of the Holiness Movement. That is one of the reasons I believe dressing well was so important to me. I made sure through those years that I looked like the other cultural winners in my society.

I knew, however, that Coach Ring cared about me. He expected a lot from me and I gave it to him. I faithfully did the drills he gave me. I would play what we called "Around the World." I would go around what today is the three-point line until I could hit ten baskets in a row from each position. I would pretend that a defender was in my face and figure out how to get the ball up and away while protecting it. I was not a quick player, so I learned fadeaway shots. I could move to my right or left and maintain my accuracy. I found ways to get open and get my shot off. I played against the best collegiate players in the US, and it was rare for them to block one of my shots. I developed a quick release, which made me as a player. I could shoot fast under very difficult pressure and consistently make the shots. My long-term goal was a college scholarship, but my immediate motivation was to please my coach.

When I became a believer, growing up without a father made it difficult for me to relate to God as my Father in heaven, so I wasn't focused on pleasing him. I related better to Jesus. Because he is God in the flesh, it is easier to understand what he is like. But when Dr. Charles Farah, a theological professor at ORU, began to disciple me, I began to develop the kind of close relationship to God that Jesus had with his Father. Dr. Farah took an interest in my roommate and me and offered to spend time with us, teaching us how to study Scripture and memorize Bible verses. He taught us the virtue of a personal devotional life. This was a goal that I could strive toward and use my discipline to accomplish. I excelled at it because it fit my worldview, which thrived on structure. Dr. Farah sometimes had me address his classes, and he used me as a good example of how to have a quiet time.

However, I confused a disciplined quiet time with a relationship to God. I went through the disciplines of study, prayer, memorization, meditation, and journaling, but when I was done I didn't feel as though I had spent time alone with a person. It wasn't anything like the relationship Jesus had with his Father—time spent talking and listening. I was drawn to Jesus' words to the church at Laodicea: "Look! I stand at the door and knock. If you hear my

89

voice and open the door, I will come in, and we will share a meal together as friends."[9] Previously, all my attention around this verse had been focused on the door, yet the last part of the verse says that "we will share a meal together as friends." I hadn't given much thought to what would happen once Jesus sat down for the meal. What would we talk about? In later years I learned that the way someone demonstrated that they had forgiven you was to have a meal with you. This is what Jesus is saying to the ancient world in which he lived: "I have forgiven you; let's eat."

As I reflected on Jesus' conversation with his Father in the garden, it seemed that they enjoyed each other's company and neither attempted to fix the other. Isn't that how friendship works? We can't relax and be friends with someone who is always trying to fix us. This dynamic always creates tension and erodes the relationship, whether between spouses, parents and their kids, or friends. I realized that if I was to have a meaningful prayer life, I needed to accept that Jesus wasn't trying to fix me. I needed to believe that what he said about accepting me was true — that he loved me completely and that his Father loved me as much as he loved his own Son. Then I wouldn't spend all my time with God confessing my sin, crying "woe is me." When I am with a friend, we catch up on our lives, talk about mutual interests, laugh about our foibles, and freely share our innermost thoughts, without fear of reprisal. This understanding transformed my conversations with God and changed how I saw him. Consequently I started wanting to please him more.

Nowadays, my favorite way to think of prayer is Jesus and me talking about what we are doing together. In this way I stay connected to the other world, the kingdom not of this world. This enables me to be a leader who is connected to my leader and to see the world the way he does.

# Jesus Taught His Disciples His Worldview

Let's return to that significant conversation Jesus had with his Father the night before his crucifixion. After telling the Father that he wanted to return to him and be glorified, Jesus talked with him about the disciples:

> I have revealed you to those whom you gave me out of the world. They were yours; you gave them to me and they have obeyed your word. Now they know that everything you have given me comes from you. For I gave them the words you gave me and they accepted them. They knew with certainty that I came from you, and they believed that you sent me.[10]

Jesus had taught his followers about the joy of relationship with his Father, so he was confident that they too had a worldview that valued the Father's agenda more than personal comfort and safety. That's why he was able to tell the Father that his disciples were ready for the mission. He was saying, "They now know you. They believe. They are ready to go." He said this *knowing that in a few hours Judas would betray him and the rest would flee in fear.* In other words, according to Jesus, being ready to go out and accomplish the mission God has for you doesn't mean passing every test. This is a significant point for the Christian leader. All of us live in a crucible of spiritual confusion and conflict. A good survival technique is to seek God's kingdom and God's ways with all our hearts, knowing that we will make mistakes. Our constant prayer must be, *God, this is what you called me to, this is what you want. I will faithfully stay in it when there is clarity, when there is fog, when there is discouragement, and when there is celebration and victory. Amen.*

I have trained a number of men to teach others and then sent them out. They sometimes stumble. They call me for help. They forget what they have been taught. They make mistakes. That, however, doesn't mean they were not ready to be sent out. It only means they are human and at different levels of competence. The more they are active in mission, the faster they learn and the more competent they become. The readiness of our followers has to do with what is in their hearts. It is about their commitment to Christ and the relationship they have with you as their leader; everything else is detail.

Once Jesus told the Father that the disciples were ready, he seemed to officially turn them back over to his Father and to their assigned mission.

> I pray for them. I am not praying for the world, but for those you have given me, for they are yours. All I have is yours, and all you have is mine. And glory has come to me through them. I will remain in the world no longer, but they are still in the world. ... Protect them by the power of your name, the name you gave me, so that they may be one as we are one.[11]

Jesus put his disciples, the ones who would carry on his mission, in a special category. They would have the burden of sacrificing themselves in the hostile world that was about to kill him. History tells us that all the disciples but John were executed in one form or another — but not before they carried out their roles as evangelists or made many disciples who carried on the mission.

Jesus wanted his disciples to know that in the midst of their failings and challenges, God was watching, caring for, and protecting them. So in their hearing he prayed for his disciples' protection, the same protection God had provided him until it was time for him to sacrifice his life. He didn't pray that they would evade all harm. In fact, he had earlier warned Peter that at times man's efforts thwart God's purpose.[12]

Dietrich Bonhoeffer understood this dynamic. The Nazis had

closed the seminary where he was teaching, and he realized that they would promptly send the young students to the most dangerous fighting. In a letter to them he wrote,

> God reminds those of you who are out on the front to remain prepared.... To be sure, God shall call you, and us, only at that hour that God has chosen. Until that hour, which lies in God's hand alone, we shall all be protected even in greatest danger; and from our gratitude for such protection ever new readiness surely arises for the final call.[13]

The faithful disciple can be sure that, regardless of the time of our departure, it will be in sync with God's plan for us.

Jesus had developed and nurtured the same connection of intimacy and trust with his disciples that he had with his Father. He knew that the time had come when that trust would be tested; he was also sure that they would stay the course.

Discipleship is rooted in trust. When trust is not developed between the leader and the followers, leadership breaks down and spiritual causes fall flat from one spiritual generation to the next. I say "spiritual generation" because the age difference between Jesus and his youngest follower was no more than ten years. Most of the criticism of classic discipleship has said, "It's just too programmed. People are just finishing curricula. It's too organized and predictable." This is misguided. Not only that, but this perception has made the problem worse by encouraging Christian leaders to discard organization, curricula, covenants, and forms of accountability. We need lifelong accountability and structure. Living in covenantal community is not a temporary arrangement because of the challenge of assimilating its lessons into your daily life. The secret to staying the course is to never leave covenantal community; the configuration of members and places may change, but the structure and covenants will continue to build and nurture trust.

Discipleship has broken down because we haven't been using Jesus as our model for leadership and done what he did or what he taught. Replication was a crucial part of Jesus' worldview. Jesus invested a lot of time in his followers. He patiently guided, chided, instructed, and showed them how to do ministry. There was tension and challenge in the relationship, but he loved them and gave them his best. His plan to make disciples depended on those disciples making other disciples. If his disciples were not able to release more disciples into mission, then this prayer in the garden was the end of the line. Much of our contemporary discipleship has lacked this relational commitment to spend time together outside of meetings and to live together in community.

Jesus' behavior revealed his worldview. He valued the Father's agenda more than a hassle-free life. He passed on to his disciples the worldview that connection with the Father is fundamental to accomplishing the mission. He taught them technique, but his relationship with them wasn't technique-driven. He taught them to pray, heal, and preach, but the skills took a backseat to the relationship, which drove the agenda. His followers failed when they fled, but they showed up at the mountain where he had told them to go, and they worshipped him, even with some doubt. They obeyed him and waited in the upper room for the Holy Spirit to appear. But once the Spirit arrived, they went out and did what Jesus had taught them. Like Jesus, they loved their lives, yet they were willing to lay them down for another reality, a world that most couldn't see, taste, or feel. The disciples' relationship with God the Father trumped everything else. Because of this worldview, they, like Jesus, were able to lay aside privilege and safety.

Thus far we've discussed what our worldview as Christian leaders needs to lay hold of and what is included. But now we'll look at what we need to let go, to voluntarily release.

# Jesus Did Not Demand the Respect Due Him

There is an athletic axiom that says, "If you can do it, it's not bragging." Respect is the coin of the realm in professional sports. Every tussle on the field or in the court has to do with respect. In many cases the respect players want for themselves is not warranted because the players are conceited. *Conceit* by definition is to think more of yourself than is appropriate.

Jesus had no conceit in him. It would be one thing if he were *not* God and had insisted on being treated as a god. But he *was* God; yet he didn't insist that others respect him for who he was. The following verse captures an important aspect of Jesus' worldview: "[Jesus], being in very nature God, did not consider equality with God something to be used to his own advantage."[14]

Sadly, too many Christian leaders are enamored with their own importance, intelligence, and skills. They are preoccupied with being treated properly both at work and in social situations.

Listen to how Jesus talked with his Father about his followers and their future:

- I have guarded them.
- I taught them so they would be filled with joy.
- The world hates them because they do not belong to the world, just as I do not belong to the world.
- I gave myself as a holy sacrifice so they can be made holy by your truth.
- I am praying not only for these disciples, but also for all who will ever believe in me through their message.
- I pray that they will all be one, just as you and I are one — as you are in me, Father, and I am in you. And may they be in us so that the world will believe you sent me.[15]

But the ultimate act of selflessness has to be his statement, "May they experience such perfect unity that the *world will know that you sent me and that you love them as much as you love me.*"[16] Jesus did not demand an exclusive relationship with his Father. He asked his Father to love his disciples at the same level the Father already loved him. This was the most important and precious relationship that Jesus had, yet he didn't insist on exclusive rights to his Father's love.

Let's try to put this into an earthly perspective. The marriage vows state, "Will you have this woman to be your wife; to live together in the covenant of marriage? Will you love her, comfort her, honor and keep her, in sickness and in health; and, forsaking all others, be faithful to her as long as you both shall live?"[17] It is clear that the man taking this vow is giving preeminence to his wife; there will be no rivals. But then along come children and both husband and wife grant permission to each other to love the children as fully as they love each other. Any parent can tell you that you can't compare the love you feel for your spouse to the love you have for your children. Part of family pathology is when there is rivalry and jealousy with spouses or children. There is one thing we know for sure. The closer we get to the mind of Christ on this issue, the better it will be for all those whom we love.

## So What?

A Christian leader's worldview matters, as it determines what actions that leader will take. When we have a worldview that says the kingdom of God governs us, it revolutionizes what we do. I have not always had this worldview and consequently have at times failed to complete the mission God gave me. Here's a case in point.

There we sat late on a Sunday night, the president of my denomination and me. I poured out my heart about how awful my church was. I was struggling with my competitive nature; I needed to succeed to meet my own ego needs. But I also wanted out in the worst way. I was desperate for some help. The president listened patiently, and when he spoke, he surprised me. "Bill," he spoke softly, "you are a good young man, one of our best, and we will always be able to find a place for you." That was a life-altering statement. He was focusing on me and my welfare rather than on the future of that church. It was very godlike, and I realized I wouldn't be a failure if I left. At the same time, I was committed to winning, to taking down the evil in the church. I decided to stay and fight it out.

Sometime later all the dynamics collided. It was one of those church meetings from hell. After years of conflict, I had thought we had worked it through and that people were tired of the fighting, bickering, gossip, and slander. But that night I found that the root of bitterness never tires; it has a never-ending energy and appetite for hurting others. When the candidates for church office came up, I was confident that we had a wonderful slate of nominees. But when the moment came for nominations from the floor, name after name was suggested. It was clear — a special-interest group had planned its counterattack. Suddenly we had an entire slate of new nominees who had given their prior permission to create the havoc. I was stunned but did appreciate the Enemy's perseverance. I collected my thoughts, and two weeks later I resigned. People wanted to know why. I confessed that my family had been miserable for the three years we had been there. After I left the room, the meeting got loud and rabid. My fans wanted to know who gave me trouble; they were taking names. The next day a representative approached me with a proposal to entice me to stay that involved getting rid of everyone who had given me trouble and rewriting the church's constitution. The problem was, I didn't like the "prize." I didn't like the way it was won, and I knew that some of what they promised me wasn't even legal. I realized then that this was no way to get my way. I walked away.

If my worldview had been like Jesus' worldview as revealed in his prayer, I would have given myself as an offering to that congregation. Only God would have been able to release me from his call. Looking back, I believe I failed to complete the mission God had given me at that church. I could have stayed as a servant, but I wasn't that committed to them, to the church, and to the ways of Jesus. I will never know what God may have done. A leader's worldview matters.

# The Humble Leader

## REHABILITATE WHAT YOU THINK OF YOURSELF

He made himself nothing by taking the very nature of a servant, being made in human likeness. And being found in appearance as a man, he humbled himself by becoming obedient to death — even death on a cross!

Philippians 2:7 – 8

If anyone would like to acquire humility, I can, I think, tell him the first step. The first step is to realise that one is proud. And a biggish step, too. At least, nothing whatever can be done before it. If you think you are not conceited, it means you are very conceited indeed.

C. S. Lewis, *Mere Christianity*

**HUMILITY DOES NOT** come naturally to us. What's natural is treating ourselves in the most generous way possible. And if we can surround ourselves with an entourage of lies about how great we are, so much the better. Even Jesus' disciples argued among themselves as to which one of them was the greatest. There is refreshing honesty in their debate; these were men of little pretense. They were angry with James and John for attempting to garner special privilege from Jesus. Jesus taught them the foolishness of such debates.

> You know that those who are regarded as rulers of the Gentiles lord it over them, and their high officials exercise authority over them. Not so with you. Instead, whoever wants to become great among you must be your servant, and whoever wants to be first must be slave of all. For even the Son of Man did not come to be served, but to serve, and to give his life as a ransom for many.[1]

I can relate to the disciples' struggle with humility. Years ago I was quite flummoxed by some of my congregation's complaints that my books were on display in a showcase in the church lobby. People in the congregation were saying things like, "He is just promoting himself and it proves that he is arrogant." I was upset, hurt, and frustrated, because it had not been my idea in the first place. Someone had suggested to me that I do this. It seemed like a good idea, as it helps sometimes for people to know that their pastor has succeeded in something. The staff discussed whether we should take the display down. But I didn't want to take it down. I was angry. What if we gave in to every pathological drama that goes on in people's wee little heads? After I calmed down, it occurred to me that I was behaving like a buffoon potentate, demanding that proper homage be paid to me.

The Christian's struggle to be humble is amplified by the fact that we do not live in a humble culture. Yes, there are pockets of humility, but humility is not the foundation of the modern culture as it once was. One of the most striking examples of how our culture has changed in this regard can be seen in our country's attitude about winning World War II. Not long ago, a PBS special aired a radio broadcast from V-J Day in 1945, when we celebrated winning the war. Many famous stars were on the program, including Frank Sinatra, Marlene Dietrich, Jimmy Durante, Dinah Shore, Bette Davis, Lionel Barrymore, and Cary Grant. I was struck by the tone of self-effacement and humility. The Allies had secured one of the noblest military victories in history and yet there were no chest bumps. No one was erecting triumphal arches. Bing Crosby said, "All anybody can do is thank God it's over. Today our deep down feeling is one of humility."[2] The actor Burgess Meredith read this passage from the famous war correspondent Ernie Pyle: "We won this war because our men are brave and because of many things — because of Russia, England, and China and the passage of time and the gift of nature's material. We did not win it because destiny created us better than all other peoples. I hope that in victory we are more grateful than we are proud."[3] It is worth sharing David Brooks's insight about that day. He stated, "It's funny how the nation's mood was at its most humble when its actual achievements were at their most extraordinary."[4]

Despite our aversion to humility, there is no more important character trait for the Christian leader to develop. Jesus our model humbled himself, and we need to learn to do the same.

In our exploration of what it means to be humble, we will first look at what it does not mean.

# What Humility Is Not

Quite often people mistake modesty for humility. Modesty involves not bragging or self-promoting. It can also refer to the way people dress, their walk and posture, and the way they talk. For example, the Amish make it a goal to dress and act modestly — or "plain," as they call it. Evangelicals sometimes mistake passivity for humility. Some point to Jesus when he did not defend himself before Pilate, or to Philippians 2:7–8, which says that Jesus gave up his divine privileges. But if Jesus was passive, how could he have conducted a three-year ministry that pierced the heart of the religious establishment? He directly challenged them on everything, from their understanding of Scripture to the way they lived. One can't be passive and get anything done for the kingdom, particularly the Great Commission. Nor is humility the denial of your gifts and abilities — that is a lack of self-respect instead. After all, leadership requires ability. It also requires vision, conviction, and confidence.

There is a difference between arrogance and having strong convictions that cause you not to compromise in certain cases. We can see this difference in the lives of Generals Douglas MacArthur and Dwight Eisenhower. Both men are giants of history; both were key military figures in leading America to victory in the Second World War. Both graduated from West Point. But that is where the similarity ends.

Eisenhower became the thirty-fourth president of the United States. MacArthur wanted to be president, but because of arrogance and insubordination, he lived out his life as an exiled warrior in a suite at New York City's Waldorf Astoria Hotel. He was honored by the nation but was never trusted because of his vanity. Eisenhower was a workhorse soldier, MacArthur a show horse. MacArthur was dangerously ambitious but respected for his military strategy. Author Michael Korda wrote, "MacArthur was wealthy, socially and politically well connected, famous, glamorous, eccentric, deeply theatrical, patrician, a shameless old-fashioned snob, a military aristocrat, and a reckless hero."[5] President Truman fired him for insubordination during the Korean War. Most discussions with MacArthur were more like monologues. He often referred to himself in the third person, as if he were a deity. In *American Caesar*, biographer William Manchester wrote this of MacArthur:

> He was a great thundering paradox of a man, noble and ignoble, inspiring and outrageous, arrogant and shy, the best of men and the worst of men, the most protean, most ridiculous, and most sublime. No more baffling, exasperating soldier ever wore a uniform. Flamboyant, imperious, and apocalyptic, he carried the plumage of a flamingo, could not acknowledge errors, and tried to cover up his mistakes with sly, childish tricks. Yet he was also endowed with great personal charm, a will of iron, and a soaring intellect. Unquestionably he was the most gifted man-at-arms this nation has produced.[6]

MacArthur was brave. He sought death on the battlefield. Much like George Patton, he insisted on being taken to the front lines and on occasion took enemy fire. Yet he considered himself above those in authority over him, even the commander in chief. MacArthur was a great man, but pride and arrogance kept him from being even more useful.

Eisenhower was intelligent, disciplined, and hardworking. He grew up on a farm in Kansas where he lived a simple life. He was ordinary at West Point; his academics were not first-rate. He knew his place and served with humility. He labored for many years in an army that didn't allow him to lead men into battle. An outstanding administrator, he worked his way up the ranks by being faithful and trustworthy, but he was frustrated with his assignments.

This was no truer than when he was given the job in 1928 to write a guidebook of American battle monuments of Europe, a task he did in his usual excellent way but without enthusiasm. In 1941 when "Ike" was appointed Supreme Allied Commander in Europe, there was great surprise because he had no battlefield experience and General George Marshall wanted the job. Eisenhower had many critics, but even they praised his fairness, energy, patience, common sense, and authority. Above all they heralded his matchless ability to deal with even the most difficult of prima donnas, including Field Marshal Bernard Montgomery, rival French generals Charles de Gaulle and Henri Giraud, and Winston Churchill.

Eisenhower knew how to "keep his eye on the ball," a favorite phrase of his. His orders were simple: "You will enter the continent of Europe and, in conjunction with the other United Nations, undertake operations aimed at the heart of Germany and the destruction of her armed forces."[7] Of course, it was over two years before D-Day was possible and three years until victory was attained. Eisenhower made decisions, including the decision for the Allies to invade France on D-Day, in a collaborative environment. He was not required to consult with anyone, but he had learned the value of teamwork, of listening to others, and of treating his commanders with respect. He showed humility in his relationships and didn't seek glory.

In the event that the D-Day invasion failed, Eisenhower wrote the following statement:

> Our landings have failed and I have withdrawn the troops. My decision to attack at this time and place was based on the best information available. The troops, the air and the Navy did all that bravery could do. If any blame or fault attaches to the attempt it is mine alone.[8]

Not many other leaders would have been willing to take full responsibility for a failure on such a global scale. One word describes the note and the man: humility.

## A Revolutionary Quality

The Greek word for humility is *tapeinos*; in Latin it's *humilitas*. Both can mean "to be made low or to lower oneself." I propose that for the Christian leader, humility *is sacrificing or lowering oneself for the benefit of others*. It is contentment and joy when you are not the focus, when you are overlooked, when no rewards are being passed out.

We see this in Eisenhower, but we can see it even more in Jesus. When it came time to die, he struggled, but what kept him on track for fulfilling his mission was his humble nature and the relationship he had to his own community, the Trinity. He wanted to please the Father and the Holy Spirit. Jesus willingly lowered himself so that others might be lifted up and live.

We tend not to appreciate how foreign humility was to the people of Jesus' day. The society in which he lived did not honor humility; in fact, it was considered immoral.

Mediterranean societies, including Israel, were honor-shame cultures. A significant question for any family member was, "Does your life bring honor to our family?" It was considered good form for generals and kings to write about themselves in glowing terms, to puff their biographies, and to discount any weaknesses or mistakes. People were expected to lower themselves before kings, who were at times considered to be gods, but never to an equal. And it would have been considered out of the question to lower oneself before someone of a lower class. It was simply not done; it was considered morally suspect.

In this honor-shame environment, Jesus' humility was radical.

He said, "Come to me, all you who are weary and burdened, and I will give you rest. Take my yoke upon you and learn from me, for I am gentle and humble in heart, and you will find rest for your souls. For my yoke is easy and my burden is light."[9] To hear most Christians tell it, being a Christian is hard, but Jesus claimed that his yoke, or being his disciple, was easy. He was speaking to those for whom life was a terrible burden and anything but easy. He was doing something that no one would do in that honor-shame-based society — invite the powerless into more powerlessness, and call it easy.

If anyone had street credibility on making something difficult seem easy, however, it was Jesus. He was God, yet he clothed himself in humanity. This choice placed severe limits on someone who had existed outside of time and space, outside of any limitations, outside of suffering, death, abuse, and triviality. In coming to earth, he acquired them all. And only because he was humble of heart was he willing to do so, and to take his life as a man to its ignominious and glorious end. Jesus is proof that it is possible to live a contented life. He told his followers, "Join me, yoke up; we will do this together."

Jesus said his disciples are to be servants. Being a servant is part of what it means to be a Christian leader. Our leader came not to be served, but to serve. We are to do the same.

# Seeking Humility

Here are some suggestions for seeking humility, for learning how to lower yourself for the benefit of others. I say "seek" because there is a dimension in the seeking that is completely a work of God's grace. He builds it into a willing heart.

## Choose Humility

Humility is something you choose; it is not something you try. As Peter Wagner wrote, "Humility is a matter of personal choice. If you are [humble], it is because you have decided that you will be humble. If you are not, it is because you have not decided to be humble."[10]

Of all the disciples who could have talked about this character trait, Peter put it most practically: "All of you, clothe yourselves with humility toward one another."[11] Peter was infamous for a lack of humility in his early days, but by the time he penned these words, he had lived another thirty years. For most of those years, he was filled with the Holy Spirit. He had been persecuted and made mistakes, and he became a humble man. He spoke of humility as something we can put on. Just as we intentionally select our clothes and put them on every day, so we are to don humility every day. Peter spoke of our humility in relation to others. A character trait is useful only when it is testable in relation to others. For example, many people are in love with the idea of love. They dream of meeting just the right person and of marriage and children. The idea is a good one, but love is irrelevant unless it becomes an action that benefits another. God's love is irrelevant apart from his acts of love. Humility is irrelevant apart from how we act in relation to other people. Peter was saying that we are to consider the people in our lives every day and to intentionally act in humility toward them. In other words, to lower ourselves to take action that will benefit them.

I am gradually growing in humility. My wife has said to me, "Bill, when we were first married you were very selfish. You have made great progress. Now you are just selfish." She is smiling when she says it, usually in the company of others for effect, but she has more than forty years of experience to back up her claim. I have made progress in becoming humble, but that progress has been gradual. It has been a product of positive events and difficult trials.

Many forces have converged over the years to create a more humble and sacrificial spirit in me. I still say to Jane, "Don't ask me if I want to empty the dishwasher; tell me you want me to, or I need to. Because I don't think I will ever get to the 'I want to clean the kitchen' level of marital delight."

The decision to be humble is a lifelong one, much like deciding to follow Christ. But as in following Christ, every day is a series of choices. And those choices create something called character. C. S. Lewis wrote, "Every time you make a choice you are turning the central part of you ... into something a little different from what it was before.... Each of us at each moment is progressing to the one state or the other ... either into a heavenly creature or into a hellish creature."[12]

## Don't Let Crowds Define You

I have found it a near impossibility to identify my motivation as a leader. If I am excited about a big crowd, is it because I am rejoicing in people hearing the message or because I am thrilled they came to hear me? I think it is both, and both can be good. Because of my theological convictions that people need Christ, I am excited when many people will hear the message. I am also deeply satisfied that I get to be a part of delivering the message, and the crowd makes me feel good. God made me to feel good when many others seem to be interested in what I have to say. God made me to experience pleasure, to be pleased when good things happen. Such is the joy of life. But the ego whispers, "You did it. You are good, and boy, these people are lucky to have you." If we don't put the ego in check, we can take the credit rather than remember God's mission and our part in it.

The ego can be just as dangerous when something happens that diminishes our sense of significance. I recall an area-wide seminar in Freeport, Illinois, which was to be held on a Friday night and Saturday in a seven-hundred-seat theater. The area had been canvassed, newspaper ads had run for two weeks, announcements had been made on local radio stations, and flyers had been passed out in all local churches. The only problem was that no one could control the weather. I sat in the Minneapolis airport, delayed five hours by a snowstorm. I arrived so late that the Friday evening meeting had to be cancelled. The sponsors who picked me up at the airport thought this was fine; the place would be packed the next morning.

Next morning, four senior citizens showed up and sat on the front row. It was to be a seven-hour seminar. The pastor asked me if I wanted to continue. I swallowed hard and said, "Of course, we should do so." I spent that day with those four people. I stood on the front of the stage, they sat on the first row of the seven-hundred-seat hall, and I gave them the entire seminar. One person left after lunch; indigestion was the excuse. It was a test of my motivation; it also knocked a lot of ego out of me. Crowds are addictive. The pleasure of holding a large crowd in your hand is a sensation that rings every pleasure bell; one's brain is splashed with endorphins. The raw power you feel, the power to manipulate, can be dangerous.

Not much has been written about the danger of crowds, except for what Eugene Peterson has noted. In a letter to a pastor leaving a small congregation for a larger one, Peterson wrote:

> Every time the church's leaders depersonalize, even a little, the worshipping/loving community, the gospel is weakened. And size is the great depersonalizer. Kierkegaard's criticism is still cogent: "the more people, the less truth." ...
>
> Classically, there are three ways in which humans try to find transcendence — religious meaning, God meaning — apart from God as revealed in the cross of Jesus: through the

ecstasy of alcohol and drugs, through the ecstasy of recreational sex, through the ecstasy of crowds. Christian leaders frequently warn against the drugs and the sex, but, at least in America, almost never against the crowds. Probably because they get so much ego benefit from the crowds.

But a crowd destroys the spirit as thoroughly as excessive drink and depersonalized sex. It takes us out of ourselves, but not to God, only away from him. . . . We hunger to escape the dullness, the boredom, and the tiresomeness of me. We can escape upward or downward. . . . A crowd is an exercise in false transcendence upward, which is why all crowds are spiritually pretty much the same, whether at football games, political rallies, or church.

So why are we pastors so unsuspicious of crowds, so naive about the false transcendence that they engender? . . . I really do feel that crowds are a worse danger, far worse, than drink or sex, and pastors may be the only people on the planet who are in a position to encourage an imagination that conceives of congregation strategically not in terms of its size but as a congenial setting for becoming mature in Christ in a community, not a crowd.[13]

I have often let crowds define me. If the crowd was large, then I was large; if small, then I was diminished. The most difficult time for me as a pastor was the time period on a Sunday morning, when the size of crowd had yet to be determined. This time period began fifteen minutes before a service and lasted for fifteen minutes into the service. Afterward, it was a good or bad Sunday, based on attendance. Crowd size didn't just define me, it owned me. I am not alone in this. Crowd size is the most powerful emotional aphrodisiac for a speaker. If Peterson's words mean anything, they mean that a crowd kills personhood and community. The ups and downs of a pastor's emotions should be determined by healthy signs of community that lead to Christlikeness in congregants, no matter the size of the church.

Humility is an acknowledgement that we are dependent on God. When we decide to live for God and to live for others, then we are no longer a slave to the crowd and its whims. This kind of living is challenging. Sometimes our motives are good and our focus is right, but we can slip easily into a carnal mode. I often laugh at the professional athlete who struts his stuff after scoring a meaningless touchdown at the end of the game when his team is behind thirty points. What makes it sad and unseemly is that he seems to not know the score. This athlete is celebrating self—as are Christian leaders who make ministry about how they feel and what is good for them rather than about the mission and pleasing the Father. These leaders celebrate their public successes, even though their congregation is not in unity or introducing people to Christ. They may be winning, their career may be winning, but their ministry and the Great Commission are losing.

## Be Teachable

Another way to cultivate humility is to be teachable. The essence of discipleship is to be a learner. Jesus said, "Everyone who is fully trained will be like their teacher"[14] and "Teach these new disciples to obey all the commands I have given you."[15] These foundational teachings require humility. Without humility a follower of Christ cannot be touched deeply by Christ.

Spend time in prayer, not in long drawn-out sessions pleading with God to make you humble, but in quiet conversation with him, acknowledging that you and God are working on this trait, side by side, as friends. Read the Bible often. Live in community, where people know your sins, and continue every day to ask God to teach you how to be his follower. Look for places to be humble.

# Don't Expect to Get Anything Out of It

One of the first statements a group of apprentice leaders hears from me is, "Don't expect to get anything out of this." I want to shock them, to challenge the very thing they are thinking. They have agreed to enroll in a spiritual community for one year and they have high expectations of what it means to lead. I go on to give my reason for saying this. "What if Jesus would have made his decision for incarnation based on what he would get out of it?" There was nothing in it for him. He was already self-sufficient and was in perfect celestial bliss in the triune community with God the Father and God the Holy Spirit. Of course, people who are in discipleship will get something out of it and indeed it will transform their lives. But the reason they enter into discipleship is to be like their leader. Jesus came to serve; he came to give. He suffered and it was rough.

What we get out of being a leader is personal transformation as we serve others. Very few Christian leaders get the rewards that society extols, such as money and fame. Some do, and it can be dangerous for them. Money and fame distract us from loving what God loves. What we get out of our position of leadership is the personal satisfaction of being able to say, "I have fought the good fight, I have finished the race, I have kept the faith."[16] What Paul got out of his ministry was the joy down deep inside that he had pleased Christ, his leader. Such knowledge is more than enough.

# Forget about Humility

Don't constantly evaluate how you are doing. C. S. Lewis put it this way:

> Do not imagine that if you meet a really humble man he will be what most people call "humble" nowadays: he will not be a sort of greasy, smarmy person, who is always telling you that, of course, he is nobody. Probably all you will think

about him is that he seemed a cheerful, intelligent chap who took a real interest in what *you* said to *him*. If you do dislike him it will be because you feel a little envious of anyone who seems to enjoy life so easily. He will not be thinking about humility: he will not be thinking about himself at all.[17]

Jesus was a man for others; as his disciples we live for others. Humility is living for others.

# Humility Helps People Trust You

When you demonstrate that you want the best for them, people will follow you. It causes them to believe your message, to like you, and to want to please you. Living for others has been a struggle for me because I don't always trust people's judgment. I also don't want to submit myself to them because I want to reserve my option to bail out if I don't like the organizational results.

On one occasion, I debated whether to resign from a church because I wasn't sure if my work there was finished. Trusted friends counseled me to stay and to set aside my ministry to the larger church in order to establish in the mind of my local church members that I was committed to them first and foremost. I trusted those who counseled me, but I decided to leave because I didn't trust the corporate heart of the congregation. Through the prophet Jeremiah, God had said, "The heart is deceitful above all things and beyond cure. Who can understand it? 'I the LORD search the heart and examine the mind, to reward each person according to their conduct, according to what their deeds deserve.' "[18] I could not bring myself to trust their corporate heart; I could not even trust my own heart in the matter. The only thing I could trust was God's heart, and I flung myself into his care for the remainder of my days.

# Life in the Middle

Let me close this discussion on humility by saying that I believe all serious Christian leaders live in the middle between pride and humility. I am dubious of the "all or nothing" advocates. Take for example Andrew Murray's classic, *Humility*. He wrote in absolute categories; his sentences don't seem to leave room for living:

> Pride must die in you, or nothing of heaven can live in you.... Humility must sow the seed, or there can be no reaping in heaven. Look not at pride only as an unbecoming temper, nor at humility only as a decent virtue: for the one is death, and the other is life; the one is all hell, the other is all heaven. So much as you have of pride within you, you have of the fallen angel alive in you; so much as you have of true humility, so much you have of the Lamb of God within you.[19]

Not much room for the way life is really lived. Neither do I think Paul's teaching in Philippians 4:6 — "Do not be anxious about anything, but in every situation, by prayer and petition, with thanksgiving, present your requests to God" — means that a Christian will never have anxiety. It is not as if we live in one of two states, either the state of anxiety or the state of zero anxiety. Paul was saying that we live with anxiety and we manage that anxiety through prayer. Similarly, we live life with a dash of pride here and a splash of humility there. So learn to live with some anxiety about your humility. God chose Peter, the least humble and most reckless of his disciples, to lead his church. Peter gave his life as a flawed man who lived in the knowledge that he was utterly dependent upon God. That, my friends, is the essence of humility.

# Becoming Something Else

## REHABILITATE HOW FAR YOU ARE WILLING TO GO

[Jesus], being in very nature God, did not consider equality with God something to be used to his own advantage; rather, he made himself nothing by taking the very nature of a servant, being made in human likeness. And being found in appearance as a man, he humbled himself by becoming obedient to death — even death on a cross!

**Philippians 2:6–8**

I don't know if you ... ever had a load of hay fall on you, but when they told me yesterday what happened, I felt like the moon, the stars, and all the planets had fallen on me. Don't expect too much of me.

**Harry Truman, after replacing Franklin Roosevelt as president of the United States**

**WITH LEADERSHIP COME** pressure and challenges. There are forces at work that you cannot prepare for or anticipate, and they change you into something different than you would have been otherwise. New leaders in particular don't often think that leadership will change them in radical ways that could be painful. They miss the warning to leaders that appears in James's epistle: "Not many of you should become teachers, my fellow believers, because you know that we who teach will be judged more strictly."[1] James was not referring just to clergy here. A "teacher in the church" is anyone who is called to influence others. Paul told Timothy that teaching was a primary responsibility.[2]

All leaders are required to teach and all teachers are required to lead. When I think of Christian leadership, I think of teaching, both formal and informal. Teachers are powerful leaders in our culture. I refer not only to the sanctioned teachers in our churches, synagogues, temples, universities, and schools, but also to newscasters, journalists, and writers of fiction and nonfiction. They all play a part. Jesus spoke about the power of teaching. A little child had come to him, and he talked about the responsibility to that child:

> He called a little child to him, and placed the child among them. And he said: "Truly I tell you, unless you change and become like little children, you will never enter the kingdom of heaven. Therefore, whoever takes the lowly position of this child is the greatest in the kingdom of heaven. And whoever welcomes one such child in my name welcomes me. If anyone causes one of these little ones — those who believe in me — to stumble, it would be better for them to have a large millstone hung around their neck and to be drowned in the depths of the sea."[3]

We as leaders must be willing to change in order to learn how to live for others. As I tell my students, if you want to become something you have never been before, you will need to do things you have never done before. Once again, Jesus is our model in this. When God became a person, he took the definitive action of emptying himself of rights and privileges in order to serve and live for others.

## Jesus, Our Example

One of the Son of God's primary acts was to change for the benefit of others. He became something different. The conditions of a broken creation called for action, and so he changed and took on human flesh. He didn't just become a person. It was more than that. He lived an ordinary human life with its inherent limitations. For the first thirty years, Jesus lived the mundane life of a carpenter's son. Couldn't God come up with a better plan, something a bit more spectacular? Why have Jesus waste all that time making mud pies as children do, playing games, and learning to read and write? Can you imagine Jesus' first steps? His first words? The first time he was attracted to a young woman? He served years as an apprentice in the carpentry trade. I am sure Jesus was good at carpentry, but he never spoke a word about it during his public ministry.[4]

Mary knew he was special and his behavior proved it. Even though Jesus was fully human, he never sinned. He never lied, cheated, or started a fight with his sisters or brothers. I am sure that at least some thought he was an odd boy. He never did any of the naughty things other kids his age did, and that kind of reputation may have created resentment in the community. This could explain why Jesus couldn't do many great works in his hometown later in his public ministry.

Because he lived a mundane daily life, Jesus can identify with all of us. This helps us to talk to him every day about our lives, troubles, and victories. It also can encourage us, because if Jesus lived an ordinary life that was godly and meant something important, then we have hope that our lives can have significance as well. Taking out the garbage, cleaning up after dinner, walking the dog, chatting with our neighbor — all have their place in the kingdom.

The Son of God was called to become something else — and he answered that call by taking on human flesh and by sacrificing himself on the cross. History is replete with men and women who have answered the call to become something else. One such leader was Harry S. Truman.

# The Man Hit on the Head with a Load of Hay

Harry S. Truman was a classic second banana. The senator from Missouri was considered the product of the powerful Tom Pendergast Missouri political machine. Pendergast chose him to run for the Senate only after three other men had turned down the invitation. Truman, who took office as "the senator from Pendergast," had an average run as senator and was not taken seriously by Washington and particularly by President Roosevelt.

Then in 1944, Roosevelt asked Truman to be his vice presidential running mate. Truman had rarely spoken to Roosevelt and hardly knew him. The only reason Roosevelt selected him was that Truman was less liberal than the then vice president, Henry Wallace. Some in the party believed that Roosevelt might not survive a fourth term; Truman let it be known he was not interested in the vice presidency. Roosevelt devised a plan to pressure him to accept the position, and on July 19 the party bosses summoned Truman to a suite in the Blackstone Hotel to listen in on a phone call that, unbeknownst to the senator, they had rehearsed in advance with the president. During the conversation, Roosevelt asked the bosses whether Truman would accept the position. When they said that he would not accept, Roosevelt angrily accused Truman of disrupting the unity of the Democratic Party in the middle of a war and then hung up. Feeling he had no choice, Truman reluctantly agreed to become Roosevelt's vice president.[5]

Truman had been vice president for eighty-two days when, on April 12, 1945, President Roosevelt died. Truman had rarely met with Roosevelt and was unaware of the Manhattan Project, which was about to test the first atomic bomb. Shortly after taking office, Truman told reporters, "Boys, if you ever pray, pray for me now. I don't know if you fellows ever had a load of hay fall on you, but when they told me yesterday what happened, I felt like the moon, the stars, and all the planets had fallen on me."[6]

Truman was president from April 12, 1945 to January 20, 1953. He was elected on his own in 1949 over Thomas Dewey in a famous razor-thin election that nearly everyone had predicted Dewey would win. The country went to bed thinking Dewey had won but awoke to a Truman miracle comeback. Not much was expected of Truman; even his own people doubted his ability. But he racked up an impressive résumé as president. He made the decision to drop the first-ever atomic bombs to end the war with Japan, he oversaw the Marshall Plan to rebuild war-torn Europe, he helped create the United Nations, and he stood strong against Soviet expansion, in part by implementing the Berlin Airlift. Moreover, when most of the world would not, Truman recognized Israel and stood behind its formation as a nation in 1948. Truman said of his decision to stand behind Israel:

> Hitler had been murdering Jews right and left.... I saw and I dream about it even to this day. On that account, the Jews needed some place where they could go.... It was my attitude that the American government could not stand idly by while the victims of Hitler's madness were not allowed to build new lives.[7]

Truman answered the call to become something else. The aftermath of World War II called on him to take courageous action and rescue West Berlin. This was the Allied sector of the city surrounded by the new Soviet powers. Truman airlifted food and supplies into the sector for several months until the blockade ended. The aftermath also called on him to help Israel become a nation. Truman became a much stronger man in his run for reelection. He integrated the armed forces against the wishes of most in Congress.

Truman was a Southern Baptist. (I am sure they are more inclined to claim him now than they were then.) He fired General MacArthur, which may have been his most courageous act after his decision to drop the atomic bomb. Of this decision he said, "I fired him because he wouldn't respect the authority of the President."[8] After firing MacArthur, Truman's approval ratings hit a new low and there were calls for his impeachment. MacArthur returned to the United States and gave a historic speech to Congress. Truman didn't even watch it; he met with the secretary of state and took a nap.

Truman was politically incorrect in an age of rampant political incorrectness. That is why he was respected then and brings a smile to our faces now. Even though he was a bit off-color, he was truly a beloved character whose popularity has soared. This was no more evident than in the dramatic success of *Truman*, David McCullough's masterful biography published in 1992.

What is to be learned about leadership from Truman? More specifically, what can the Christian leader learn from his example? Truman was transformed by the call to lead, and he led far above his natural ability. His capacity was greater than even he imagined. Isn't this true for the Christian leader as well?

There are far more Christian leaders in the secular realm than in the religious arena. If America has approximately 338,000 churches and we assign an average of two clergy to each, it means we have fewer than one million clergy. If we throw in those who are ordained and lead an organization of some kind, the numbers might be somewhere between 1.5 and 2 million.[9] This means that Christian leaders are more likely to be men and women who work outside of the church and who lead within businesses or organizations. And when they take the leadership role, like Truman, they may feel as if a load of hay has fallen on them. But the call to lead can transform them into something that otherwise would have been impossible to predict, as was the case for Truman.

# Discovering What Is in You

You don't know what you have in you until you step up, until you act in faith to obey God. I didn't know much about my leadership ability until after I became a follower of Christ. What I did know was that I was able to focus on a project and get it done, and that I was a good salesman. At age twenty I was making two hundred dollars a week, cold-calling businesses on the phone to sell them FM radio advertising when FM radio was in its infancy. That was a lot of money for a college student working a summer job. I don't know how I did it; I just did.

Many have characterized me as relentless; my wife was the first to notice this when we were dating. I kept asking her about marriage. "Yes, I know we don't have the money; we are college students. But if we did have the money, if we were a bit older, would you marry me?" I would go on like this on a regular basis. But like many leaders, I was shy and introverted. When I was in a room of people, I rarely spoke. It wasn't until a mission trip to Africa in 1968 that my life changed on this point.

On the trip, I was asked to give a sermon to some sixty-five villagers. It had never occurred to me that I would preach. I didn't think of myself in that way; I was going to be a coach. But I preached and the entire village decided to become followers of Jesus. Now, it's true that the interpreter, an African pastor, spoke longer than I did, and I am sure he had more to do with this response than I did. But I knew God had used me and I have never recovered. After that experience every other path I could have taken in life faded quickly into the background. I knew I would spend the rest of my life preaching, or, as I would describe it now, making disciples. The next day I preached in a busy bus station in Nairobi. Soon churches began asking me to speak because of my basketball talents. Then, when I became a pastor, I needed to lead. Because I was required to lead, I discovered that I could lead.

For me, and perhaps for you, Christian leadership is preter-natural. It comes from outside my nature but has become part of my nature.[10] Here's an image that depicts my relationship with leadership. It's a Sunday morning and I am in my study. I have spent an hour praying and reviewing my sermon notes. I pop a breath mint, grab the door handle, take a deep breath, put a big smile on my face, open the door, and step out to greet the public. I would rather have stayed in my study, but if I had, I wouldn't have answered God's call on my life. I wouldn't have grown, I wouldn't have become something else. I would have never loved as I love, never have hurt as I hurt. I would not have learned as much, accom-plished as much, or enjoyed life as much. Even so, I still need a little push out of my study door every day.

## Becoming Less, Being More

One of the most effective leaders I know is Lori Rinkert. Lori is a woman of many talents. She is a trained physical therapist, businesswoman, and faithful wife and mother. For years Lori has had a fruitful ministry of speaking, writing, and mentoring women. She is particularly good at training and helping women's groups do strategic planning. For a number of years she was the women's ministry director at a church I pastored. She did wonders with that ministry, and it became as influential as any ministry we had.

When Lori approached fifty years of age, she was ready to soar and become a national figure and force. But several difficult events took place in her life. The first was an automobile accident that injured her brain stem. She suffered blackouts and periods of disorientation along with severe neck pain. She underwent successful brain surgery at UCLA Medical Center, but it took a couple of years for her to heal from the trauma and to regain her energy. Then Lori's son, who was in law enforcement, was seriously injured. Lori and her husband, Dan, cared for him for over a year. During this time, Lori and Dan battled the San Diego County Planning Commission over their plans to split a lot. Because of the conflicts, they lived in a small trailer even though Dan had a well-paying job. They were nomads for several years, until the land issue was settled. Then just about the time Dan and Lori were ready to go on with their lives, her father had a serious stroke. Lori and Dan have lived with and cared for her father, nursing him back to health. Their house is basic. They don't have much furniture and sleep on air mattresses.

Lori dropped by to visit the other day; we hadn't seen her in nearly four years. We sat together for hours, remembering, laughing, crying, praying, and speaking of God's faithfulness. Lori didn't exhibit one hint of resentment, even though she has not been able to do public ministry for a while now. As a caregiver, she has no time. But I see spiritual greatness in her. Lori hasn't been speaking to large crowds lately, but she has been speaking.

Her father once was a practicing Christian, but many years ago he left his family for another woman. Now that woman has abandoned him. But Lori hasn't, and because of the sacrifice of Lori and Dan, her father is now back in Christ's fold. Not long ago, her father's sister became very ill; in fact, the family was called together to say their good-byes. At the hospital, Lori's cousin, an avowed atheist, asked Lori if God was real and if prayer worked. Lori answered affirmatively and then prayed for healing for her cousin's mom. The next day the dying woman recovered. The doctors and nurses claimed they had never seen someone recover from that particular illness. Lori could hardly believe her ears as her father witnessed to his sister and as her cousin told everyone that God was real and answered prayer.

Because Lori became something different under pressure, God was able to reach hardened hearts. Lori and Dan are a testament to how less becomes more. The entire family was transformed by Lori and Dan's love and incarnation of Christ. I believe that Lori will once again expand her public ministry, but I am uncertain whether she will ever do greater ministry than she has done over the past two years.

Make no mistake about it: Becoming less takes a toll. It did for Lori and Dan. It did for Jesus, and it will for us. Because of that, most young leaders do not willingly choose it.

# A Difference between Jesus and Us

Achieving less can be more, but this doesn't naturally occur to us, particularly when we are young. Young leaders have a great deal of optimism. They have plenty of bounce and resiliency, because there is always tomorrow, another opportunity, another position. But as the years pass and fame and fortune continue to give us the slip, we grow weary of trying to make it big. One difference between Jesus and most of us is that he *willingly* took a role that limited him. He chose to descend into greatness. He took less because it was more, and to do so was his nature. We often take less because it is all that we are offered. That has certainly been the case for me.

I have grown tired of trying to prove myself and nudge my way into a more prominent position. Prominence in my work is about being heard and being taken seriously. No significant honors have come my way—no honorary doctorates, book awards, commencement addresses, or honorary roasts. I laughingly recall the routine comedic actor Red Buttons gave at the Dean Martin Celebrity Roasts. He would question why, let's say Milton Berle, was being given a dinner in his honor. Buttons pointed out that Moses, Abraham Lincoln, and George Washington—none of these important people ever got a dinner. Then he asked, "So why is this schmuck, Milton Berle, getting a dinner?" Well, add me to the list. I've never had a dinner given in my honor. I can't even win the Layman of the Year award at my church. I had hopes of being on *Larry King Live*, but then he retired and went off the air. So it goes.

Sad, isn't it? I am like an elderly woman dressed in an evening gown waiting to be discovered by her Prince Charming. I have found solace in being loved; I am told it is much better than being famous. (I am suspicious, however, that this is what famous people tell us because they don't want to share their fame.) Several times a week, though, I do get notes, emails, voice messages, tweets, and Facebook comments like this one:

> Dear Bill,
>
> Merry and Happy! Thank you for your friendship and witness. Your work for the Lord has changed the way I look at my faith and belief and the practice of it. I have no doubt that the Father led me to your ministry of discipleship. It has changed for the better my concept of "church." It has invigorated my prayer life, and reinforced my desire to practice the disciplines that lead to effective discipleship.

Okay, notes like this are better than an honorary dinner. But I have found that becoming something else can be a rather ignominious process into which I have been dragged kicking and screaming.

# My Journey to Become Something Else

I became something else, something other than what I naturally would have become, by becoming an evangelical pastor. Do not underestimate the difficulty of the task. While I generally agree with evangelical theology, I am at odds with the evangelical subculture and its version of holiness. The office of pastor applied pressure that created in me a Christlike character. If I had not accepted the call, I would not have been changed.

Every pastor knows the restrictions of the profession. For one thing, you can't be yourself. For some of us, this is a plus, considering who we really are! A pastor has to act like an adult, even though he is tempted to put his hand under his arm and make a rude noise. On the positive side, pastors are required to take seriously people and their anger, hurt, wounds, and troubles. Caring for people creates a depth of character that would be hard to develop otherwise.

On the negative side, pastors have to put up with a lot of unholy nonsense. Every Sunday when I was pastoring, I was expected to lead the congregation in prayer in a rather priestly way. The pastoral prayer, as it was called, has now faded away in most churches. I didn't care for this ritual; the organ would play in the background for effect while I attempted to pray a really good prayer. If I could make my voice shake or conjure up a tear now and then, all the better. It made me holy.

When I first arrived at the church, there was a backlog of young couples that wanted to get married—about ten as I remember it. I began a busy season of premarital counseling. As I interviewed the couples, I learned that several of them were in a hurry to marry because of pregnancy. According to the church wedding policy, pregnant couples had to be married in the chapel. They were not allowed to be married in the sanctuary, and only immediate family members were allowed to attend the ceremony as guests. The bride was not supposed to wear a white dress. This was the penalty the couple had to pay for the pregnancy. I didn't agree with the policy because it didn't deal with the real issues—premarital sex on the part of the couple and a judgmental spirit on the part of the church.

As I quizzed the couples, I found that most of them were engaging in premarital sex. According to church policy, however, the brides-to-be who were not pregnant could have the full wedding with white dress and all. I went to the church board and explained that the sin was premarital sex—not getting pregnant—and that most of the engaged couples were having sex. I felt that to be consistent, they should have to pay the same penalty as the couples who were expecting babies. Some of the offenders were their sons and daughters. When I finished, the room was silent. I gave the board a choice. Either I could bring every case before them, one by one, or they could leave the matter to my judgment as pastor. To my great sigh of relief, they left it up to me. This was a small part of the shame-based Christianity I found in the church. These were well-intentioned people who selectively punished others for a common sin rather than seeing that the real evil was a judgmental attitude.

The dead hand of religion works this way. A healthy environment creates openness and honesty; a religious spirit creates people who are closed and dishonest. A closed, dishonest environment that punishes people who tell the truth is destructive. I disliked the pretentious spirit of folks who followed the rules on the outside but were dirty on the inside. Such included church leaders who read *Playboy* yet railed against pornography, self-righteous board members who slithered out to the local racetrack and played the ponies, and the Sunday school superintendent who smoked a joint in his garage every day to calm himself down after work. It included the church soloist, a wife and mother of two, who committed adultery with her high school sweetheart when he "just happened" to stop by one day, the junior high youth sponsor who was arrested for child molestation, church members who were arrested for solicitation of a prostitute, and the male cross-dressing Sunday school teacher. It included wife beaters and stalkers. What I marveled at was not the behavior; it was people's ability to just whistle along in life as though living two lives was normal. I am just as sinful as any of them, but in real Christian living, there is repentance, forgiveness, restoration, and living in the safety of an environment of grace. The duplicitous life of many Christians exhausted my sense of credulity; I just couldn't believe that life in Christ had to be this smarmy.

I began to see that people were stuck in these destructive patterns because they didn't know how to change. They needed an environment of grace, a place where they felt safe to confess their sins. If the Enemy can keep us isolated in our own secret compartments of private sins, then we are prisoners. The first great truth that struck me was that God treats me every day better than I deserve. We call that grace. I needed to start treating these people that way rather than being frustrated or put off by them. To do this, I had to admit to myself that I had some of the same underlying issues. While the religious structure of my profession had kept me from committing many of the hot and juicy sins, my attitude toward people who committed certain sins was just as sinful as anything they did.

If I had not been a leader, I don't think I would ever have been challenged to learn to love people the way Christ loves them. I would have felt I had the option of walking away. Becoming a leader called me to become something else. I was very young then, and I didn't get all the way there, but I made progress. The church was deeply wounded, a root of bitterness had taken hold, and many were acting out of fear and frustration. In trying to establish an environment of grace and reconciliation, I took on a great deal of criticism. I led meetings with the goal of bringing about reconciliation, only to be accused of taking sides. I had never had enemies before, at least the kind with names and faces, people with whom I had shaken hands and sat across from at church dinners. I always envisioned grand enemies like editors of newspapers, theologians, politicians, and people of importance. Mine were housewives, retired schoolteachers, housewives, insurance salesmen, housewives, janitors, and housewives. I am sure I would not have reached any kind of Christlikeness without my enemies. What a gift they were to me. I want to say, "Thank you, enemies. I want to give you a big hug." Because of their criticism, I got on my knees and prayed, *Lord, I am not afraid of any change you want to make in my life.*

Being a leader helped me begin to take ownership of the effect I was having on people. I was often driving people rather than leading them, pushing rather than pulling. So the criticism was deserved at times. Yet over time, I learned that leadership was about helping people see that Christ was the treasure, and selling everything to get him was the wisest choice anyone could make.[11]

# Preparing to Become Something Else

Even though many of the changes in our lives are due to pressures that we don't choose or expect, we can practice some basic activities to prepare ourselves for change. If you want to nurture transformation, seek God in prayer and in reading Scripture and other literature. Take time to think and pray and talk with others who are on the same journey of discipleship. Keep putting one foot in front of the other, walking in the right direction. Keep breathing spiritually, exhaling the impure and inhaling the pure. Then let life happen. With a seeking heart, you will start hearing from God.

Selling leader transformation is like selling preventive health care. We know it is good to eat right, drink plenty of water, exercise, and get enough sleep. Everyone knows healthful living can help delay or even prevent disease. But often we wait until illness strikes; then we become health conscious and join a health club. Life catches up with us. I call life "the big curriculum." Most curricula are planned. You know what you are getting into and what the point is. The "big curriculum," however, is unpredictable. It teaches us faster than any other kind. The important thing is to be ready to learn, and to have a prepared attitude that will turn all of life into a seminar on Christlikeness.

# Leadership in Hard Times

## REHABILITATE HOW MUCH YOU CAN TAKE

He humbled himself by becoming obedient to death — even death on a cross!

**Philippians 2:8**

"You don't know what you are asking," Jesus said. "Can you drink the cup I drink or be baptized with the baptism I am baptized with?" "We can," they answered. Jesus said to them, "You will drink the cup I drink and be baptized with the baptism I am baptized with."

**Mark 10:38 – 39**

The man who has not suffered, what could he possibly know, anyway?

**Rabbi Abraham Heschel**

**SOME LEADERS ARE** asked to die, others are required to live, but for most it is a little of both. All leaders are called to suffer. Speaking of his own death, Jesus said:

> The hour has come for the Son of Man to be glorified. Very truly I tell you, unless a kernel of wheat falls to the ground and dies, it remains only a single seed. But if it dies, it produces many seeds. Anyone who loves their life will lose it, while anyone who hates their life in this world will keep it for eternal life. Whoever serves me must follow me; and where I am, my servant also will be.[1]

Jesus not only suffered, he also called his disciples to suffer. All of us who follow and lead for him will suffer in various ways. Yet after all his teaching on suffering, we find Jesus on his knees in the garden of Gethsemane, asking for a way out of the suffering. Doesn't this seem a bit conflicted, particularly because Jesus knew the reasons for and answers to suffering (unlike us)? His plea for a way out of suffering seems to be an admission that suffering was not the preferred plan.

So what gives? There is room for anger here. The problem of illness and death troubles us. We never get used to it. When someone is lowered into the ground, something deep inside us cries out, "This is wrong." Christian leaders in particular must wrestle with the fact of suffering and the love of a God who lets bad things happen.

# Finding Comfort at the Cross

Nothing challenges our faith more than the death of children. We consider Herod the Great to be a monster for ordering the death of all male children two years and younger to eliminate a possible rival. But God himself ordered the death of all Egyptian firstborn sons in the first Passover to persuade Pharaoh to let the Israelites leave Egypt. Were the wails of Egyptian mothers any less horrific than those of Jewish mothers?

The novel *The Blood of the Lamb* by Peter DeVries explores the tragedy of a child's death.[2] Two-thirds of the book is about Don Wanderhope's life, doubts, and struggle with God. The last third is about his daughter Carol and her dying. Wanderhope is damaged by the death of close family members, including his wife, but finds hope in eleven-year-old Carol. She becomes ill and he takes her to the hospital, where doctors diagnose her with strep throat. Thrilled, Don takes her home. That night, with Carol curled up in her chair, Don begins to feel more positive and think more hopefully about God. Then Carol's fever and back pain return. A few days later, the doctors tell him that she has leukemia and to readmit her to the hospital.

Don goes to St. Catherine's Church to kneel and pray before St. Jude, the saint of lost causes and hopeless cases. He asks that Carol live for one year. Beside him is a boxed cake that he plans to bring to the hospital so that Carol can have a birthday party. As he is about to leave the church, a nurse enters, looking for him to tell him that Carol has developed a serious infection. Wanderhope rushes to the hospital, where the news is grim. One look at Carol and he knows it is time to say good-bye. The illness has ravaged her bloodstream and she has septicemic discolorations all over her body. When the nurse leaves the room, Wanderhope whispers quickly to Carol, "The Lord bless thee and keep thee: The Lord make his face to shine upon thee, and be gracious unto thee: The Lord lift up his countenance upon thee, and give thee peace."

A short while later, Carol dies. Stunned, Wanderhope retreats to the bar down the street and drinks until the bartender refuses to serve him any longer. When he passes St. Catherine's, he is reminded that in his haste to get to the hospital that morning, he had left Carol's cake at the church. After retrieving it and taking it outside, he turns to the crucified Christ hanging over the central doorway of the church and vents his pent-up rage and pain. The following scene, the first part of which is written in Wanderhope's voice, describes what happens next:

> Then my arm drew back and let fly with all the strength within me.... It was miracle enough that the pastry should reach its target at all, at that height from the sidewalk. The more so that it should land squarely, just beneath the crown of thorns. Then through scalded eyes I seemed to see the hands free themselves of the nails and move slowly toward the soiled face. Very slowly, very deliberately, with infinite patience, the icing was wiped from the eyes and flung away. I could see it fall in clumps to the porch steps. Then the cheeks were wiped down with the same sense of grave and gentle ritual, with all the kind sobriety of one whose voice could be heard saying, "Suffer the little children to come unto me ... for of such is the kingdom of heaven."
>
> Then the scene dissolved itself in a mist in which my legs could no longer support their weight, and I sank down to the steps. I sat on its worn stones, to rest a moment before going on. Thus Wanderhope found at that place which for the diabolists of his literary youth, and for those with more modest spiritual histories too, was said to be the only alternative to the muzzle of a pistol: the foot of the Cross.[3]

Like Wanderhope, when we are faced with such intense pain and suffering, the only place we can find hope and comfort is at the foot of the cross. Let's return for a moment to Jesus on his knees in Gethsemane. Why was he in such agony? I think it important to point out that Jesus had a perfect will to live, much more so than the normal human. Humankind's will to live is debilitated by sin, by the wear and tear of life. Jesus' will to live, however, did not diminish; he prayed that the "cup of death" would pass him by. Scripture tells us he had great drops of sweat, possibly mixed with blood. Medical doctors have commented that this is possible only if someone is in great distress.

It mystifies us that Jesus, who knew that physical death was not the end of his existence, would be so upset. If anyone ever had all the answers to suffering and death, it would have been God himself. So why was he so upset? The stock answer is that the unknown of becoming sin, of bearing sin, of taking the punishment for all sin, created the agony in Jesus. In the face of death, we too fear the unknown. The randomness of death and the senselessness of it all create a great deal of fear, doubt, anger, and depression. We can find comfort and strength in Jesus' example and teachings, and in his promise to help us cope with all the unknowns, including the greatest of all unknowns, death.

# The Challenges Suffering Presents to Christian Leaders

We tend to think that our suffering might be easier to bear if we knew the reason behind it. How often we have said or heard something like, "If I only knew why God took my son so early or why so many innocents must die so horribly, then it would be easier to bear." I don't think this knowledge would ease our pain. In fact, I think the example of Jesus in Gethsemane shows us that it would create even more angst in us. The more we know, the deeper we go into the mind of God until we lose our way in his ways, which are higher than ours and beyond our comprehension. That is why in the end, Job just shut up.[4]

Christian leaders have the burden of explaining the general cause of suffering, why things are the way they are in the world. Scripture, of course, tells us that the foundational cause of all suffering is the curse. Before the fall, man and woman were without sin and suffering. Life could have continued on that course, but it didn't. Adam, our representative, fell into sin and death and we all fell into that existence with him. Sin and suffering entered into human existence.

I recently hosted Pastor Alfred Komagum from the war-torn region of northern Uganda. Alfred lives in Kitgum, a region near the Sudanese border that was terrorized for years by a war between the Ugandan government and rebels who sought to overthrow it. The horror was made worse by Sudan's war and famines. Many children were abducted. Boys were forced to become soldiers, and girls were raped repeatedly or forced to become wives of the rebels.

We have a lot of helicopters in my part of town, and when Alfred heard them he said they reminded him of war. Alfred benefited from the remarkable work of Dame Irene Gleeson, who asked God to send her to where people were suffering the most. She sold her beach house in Sydney and moved to Kitgum. For over twenty years Irene led an elementary school of ten thousand students, many of them orphans. Fifteen years ago, Alfred worked for Irene as a carpenter; now he pastors a church of well over a thousand in Kitgum. He also leads a vocational college of fifteen hundred students and represents the future of the gospel movement in that region of Uganda.

Alfred is innocent of many of our American ways. He can't believe all the food and goods that are available here. But one thing

141

Alfred does know is suffering and death; it has been with him most of his life. Westerners struggle with suffering and evil because our culture, especially our church culture, has not faced it as the norm.

Not only must Christian leaders explain the general cause of suffering, we must also give an answer to those who accuse God of being brutal, unfair, and horribly arrogant for creating the world when he knew humankind would fall and be separated from him. I heard one skeptic ask why anyone would want to worship a God who created humanity and then let them wallow in misery for one hundred thousand years before intervening to help. In a similar vein, a friend recently said concerning her husband's illness, "I don't know if I believe in God anymore considering what he has done to me."

Are we as Christian leaders ready to lead for a God who created a world like this? Are we ready to trust him, even though he hasn't given us all the answers to our questions? For me, the most challenging part of leading has been my inability to take away the trouble in people's lives. I recall a steely, cold day many winters ago. I walked with a young couple through a deserted graveyard behind an undertaker who was carrying a small casket to a gravesite. There we stood, a young couple holding hands and a young pastor holding a Bible, praying. We were confused and numb as we laid their infant to rest.

Christian leaders always seem to end up in situations in which suffering people ask questions and depend on them for guidance. We don't struggle only with the sudden and obscene loss of those we love through war, disease, famine, and accidents; we also have struggles and troubles in our living. Leaders spend a great deal of their time dealing with dysfunctions, factions, discord, sexual deviance, and addictions. Even more challenging is the criticism sometimes leveled at us because we are trying to help. Christian leaders must come to terms not only with the suffering of others, but also with the trials, temptations, sufferings, and enemies that are peculiar to themselves. We must come to terms with the nature of the people we lead and with the God who calls us to live in that environment.

## God's Prescription for Suffering: Conversion and Community

Somewhere Western Christians got the idea that God's favor means a life free of conflict and sorrow. How many people have left a church because of the conflict they saw in the congregation? They say things like, "We can't worship here knowing what is going on." "I can't be in the same room with those people. They hurt me." Those with a consumer or entitlement mentality declare, "I must have my needs met."

Great Christian leaders help people see the world the way God sees it: broken. The order of the world has been damaged, which includes everything in the physical realm. When a tornado rips a town to shreds or a tsunami sweeps thousands away, it is part of the curse, the destruction of the paradise that once was. When the scholar and athlete gets killed in a drive-by shooting, or the wonderful Christian young man is taken because of brain cancer, it all falls under the deconstruction of humankind and of earth. These are the times when people must choose between a story of doubt and darkness or a story of hope and promise.

Conversion is key to a person's ability to come to terms with the conflict and evil in the world. Dr. Kenneth J. Surin, professor of literature at Duke University, put it this way:

> So it is conversion — which comes about when the human
> will co-operates with divine grace — that solves the "problem
> of evil."... The unconverted person's endeavors to resolve the

143

"problem of evil," no matter how sincere and intellectually gifted this person might be, are doomed ultimately to be self-defeating. Only faith in Christ makes possible the cleansing of our vision, a cleansing regarded by Augustine as the necessary preliminary to the vision of God.... Without [such] conversion, the very *process* of seeking an answer to the question "whence is evil?" will be undermined by the distorted thinking of a crippled intellect.[5]

As to what Christians are to do with the problem of evil, Stanley Hauerwas noted, "Christians do not have a 'solution' to the problem of evil. Rather they have a community of care that has made it possible for them to absorb the destructive terror of evil that constantly threatens to destroy all human relations."[6] Christian leaders must lead others through the philosophical and emotional jungle that is life. While the church may not have a fully satisfying intellectual answer to suffering, it does provide a loving community to help absorb the shock and trauma of such events. As we lead people through confusing and troubled times, they find comfort in conversion to Christ and in the "community of care" he has brought into existence.

In confusing times, few people have a clear view of reality, which is why insightful leaders are so crucial during such periods. One such leader was the German pastor and scholar Dietrich Bonhoeffer.

# Dietrich Bonhoeffer:
## An Incarnational Leader

Born February 4, 1906, Bonhoeffer was one of eight children. His father, Karl, was a prominent German psychiatrist; his mother, Paula, the daughter of nobility. The Bonhoeffers were members of the elite, of the aristocracy of Berlin. Even though the family did not attend church, when he was fourteen Bonhoeffer announced he would study to be a theologian. Gifted intellectually, he acquired his PhD at age twenty-one. He was an accomplished pianist, a lover of the arts, and a man for all seasons. Bonhoeffer grew up in the same neighborhood as, and was a friend to, the world-renowned church historian Adolf von Harnack.

Bonhoeffer saw what few of his contemporaries did. He perceived the depth of evil represented by the Nazi philosophy and the sinister agenda of Adolf Hitler. Many of the older church leaders of his day were given to compromise and appeasement regarding the policies of the Third Reich. What set Bonhoeffer apart from his peers and his elders was his clarity about Jesus' teachings in the Sermon on the Mount and how they applied to the Nazis' treatment of the Jews.

On February 1, 1933, the twenty-seven-year-old Bonhoeffer gave a radio address at the Potsdammerstrasse radio station titled, "The Younger Generation's Altered Concept of Leadership." It dealt with the fundamental problems of leadership by a *Führer*.[7] It explained "how such a leader inevitably becomes an idol and a 'mis-leader.'"[8] No one knows who did it, but before Bonhoeffer finished the speech, the broadcast was cut off.

Bonhoeffer had an independence about him that demonstrated itself early in his adult life. He first went to New York City in 1930 on a fellowship to Union Theological Seminary. New York was the bastion of liberal Christianity, and Union at that time was one of its strongest bastions. Even though Bonhoeffer had been a student at Berlin University, one of the most liberal and prestigious universities in Europe, he resisted its liberal theology. He had seen how liberal theology had failed Germany in the First World War, and his view of its vacuous teachings had not changed. He wrote:

There is no theology here.... They talk a blue streak without the slightest substantive foundation and with no evidence of any criteria. The students — on the average twenty-five to thirty years old — are completely clueless with respect to what dogmatics is really about. They are unfamiliar with even the most basic questions. They become intoxicated with liberal and humanistic phrases, laugh at the fundamentalists, and yet basically are not even up to their level.[9]

He went on to complain, "In New York they preach about virtually everything; only one thing is not addressed, or is addressed so rarely that I have as yet been unable to hear it, namely, the gospel of Jesus Christ, the cross, sin and forgiveness, death and life."[10] It is difficult to appreciate how strong a will Bonhoeffer must have possessed in order to stand up against the greatest liberal minds of his time.

After a few more years of internships and the writing of a second dissertation to qualify as a lecturer at the University of Berlin, Bonhoeffer returned to New York to do a teaching tour and lecture at Union. On June 12, 1939, he arrived in New York for a second time. Yet he was uneasy. His friends had persuaded him to take refuge in America for his own safety. He had refused to be drafted into the German army and had pacifist leanings. He could no longer teach or publish in Germany, and the seminary he had started had been closed. He stayed in New York only twenty-six days. He often said there was only one important question: "What is the will of God for me here and now?" After much prayer and soul-searching, Bonhoeffer returned to Germany. He was convinced that unless he was in Germany during the trouble, he would have no right to help rebuild his country later.

From his return in 1940 until his imprisonment in 1943, Bonhoeffer traveled on church business and worked for the Abwehr, a German military intelligence organization that secretly opposed the Nazi regime. He had been hired by his brother-in-law,

Hans von Dohnanyi, because it was believed that if he worked for the Abwehr, the Gestapo would leave him alone. Bonhoeffer's role was primarily as a courier when he contacted church leaders in England to arrange a peaceful end to the war as soon as Hitler was dead. It was his knowledge of attempts on Hitler's life and his agreement with the conspiracies that led to his imprisonment.

After several attempts to kill Hitler failed, the noose around the neck of those involved in the conspiracy tightened. Some damaging files were found during a round of arrests by the Gestapo. The papers told of the plot to kill the *Führer*. Not only was Dohnanyi's name revealed, but Dietrich Bonhoeffer's was also. Around four o'clock on April 5, 1943, Bonhoeffer's father told him that two men wanted to talk to him. He took his Bible and went to see them. They escorted him to a black Mercedes. He never returned home again.

Bonhoeffer spent the next two years in prison, time by no means wasted. He worked on his magnum opus, *Ethics*, and wrote many letters to family and friends. Both manuscript and letters were edited and later released with the help of his close friend and biographer Eberhard Bethge. He longed to get out of prison, but he was resigned to the reality that he might never be released. The last two months of the war were torture for Bonhoeffer and the other political prisoners, as they were moved about the countryside. One day it seemed as if their guards would let them go; the next, they would be moved once more. This went on until the very last days of Bonhoeffer's life.

Less than twenty-four hours before he left this world, Bonhoeffer did pastoral work. On April 8, 1945, the first Sunday after Easter, he held a service in a bright schoolroom that also served as a cell. He prayed and read the verses for that day, Isaiah 53:5 ("By his wounds we are healed") and 1 Peter 1:3 ("Praise be to the God and Father of our Lord Jesus Christ! In his great mercy he

147

has given us new birth into a living hope through the resurrection of Jesus Christ from the dead").

When he finished, two men came for him. All the prisoners knew that this meant that Bonhoeffer was to be executed. Hitler was a petty man and even though he knew the war was lost, he wanted all conspirators to be put to death. A fellow prisoner said of Bonhoeffer, "He was, without exception, the finest and most lovable man I have ever met."[11] The camp doctor, Hermann Fischer-Hüllstrung, recorded his impression of Bonhoeffer just prior to his execution:

> Through the half-open door in one room of the huts I saw Pastor Bonhoeffer, before taking off his prison garb, kneeling on the floor praying fervently to his God. I was most deeply moved by the way this loveable man prayed, so devout and so certain that God heard his prayer. At the place of execution, he again said a short prayer and then climbed the steps to the gallows, brave and composed. His death ensued after a few seconds. In the almost fifty years that I worked as a doctor, I have hardly ever seen a man die so entirely submissive to the will of God.[12]

There was a quality of life inherent in Bonhoeffer that caused others to admire and follow him. It could be seen in his tough negotiations within the larger German evangelical church as he tried to persuade it to speak in defense of the Jews. It could be seen when, in his twenties, he played a significant role in the formation of the Confessing Church, a church formed in protest of the compromised German Lutheran church. It could be seen in his teachings and writings. From the lecture hall at the University of Berlin to the pages of *Discipleship* and *Life Together*, he accused the church of selling cheap grace to the masses and not standing for the oppressed. He believed that for the church to be the church, it must stand between the oppressor and the oppressed. He said that not to speak is to speak, not to act is to act. One of his most famous passages challenges us all.

> Cheap grace means grace as a doctrine, as principle, as system. It means forgiveness of sins as a general truth; it means God's love as merely a Christian idea of God.... The church that teaches this doctrine of grace thereby confers such grace upon itself. The world finds in this church a cheap cover-up for its sins, for which it shows no remorse and from which it has even less desire to be set free. Cheap grace is, thus, denial of God's living word, denial of the incarnation of the word of God. Cheap grace means justification of sin but not of the sinner. Because grace alone does everything, everything can stay in its old ways. "Our action is in vain."[13]

Bonhoeffer's modern-day biographer sums up the man's leadership with these words:

> Bonhoeffer understood that to fight evil, one must train Christians to live as Christians and learn how to pray, how to worship God and actually behave as though these things are true — not just be theoretical and theological about it.[14]

Bonhoeffer sacrificed much to lead. But he was a man very much like many of us. If there is one thing that might help us understand the inside of a man who would do such a thing, it would be his poem "Wer Bin Ich?" or "Who Am I?"

> *Who am I? They often tell me*
> *I stepped from my cell's confinement*
> *Calmly, cheerfully, firmly,*
> *Like a squire from his country-house.*
> *Who am I? They often tell me*
> *I used to speak to my warders*
> *Freely and friendly and clearly,*

*As though it were mine to command.*
*Who am I? They also tell me*
*I bore the days of misfortune*
*Equally, smilingly, proudly,*
*Like one accustomed to win.*

*Am I then really all that which other men tell of?*
*Or am I only what I myself know of myself?*
*Restless and longing and sick, like a bird in a cage,*
*Struggling for breath, as though hands were*
   *compressing my throat,*

*Yearning for colors, for flowers, for the voices of birds,*
*Thirsting for words of kindness, for neighborliness,*
*Tossing in expectation of great events,*
*Powerlessly trembling for friends at an infinite distance,*
*Weary and empty at praying, at thinking, at making,*
*Faint, and ready to say farewell to it all?*

*Who am I? This or the other?*
*Am I one person today and tomorrow another?*
*Am I both at once? A hypocrite before others,*
*And before myself a contemptibly woebegone weakling?*
*Or is something within me still like a beaten army,*
*Fleeing in disorder from victory already achieved?*
*Who am I? They mock me, these lonely questions of mine.*
*Whoever I am, Thou knowest, O God, I am Thine!*[15]

# A Bonhoeffer Moment

A Bonhoeffer moment is a time when a leader must make a decision to do something different that will cause him or her to be transformed. A leader is faced with a Bonhoeffer moment when doing the right thing is a hard, disturbing, and threatening thing. Bonhoeffer saw from the beginning that Hitler and his philosophy could not be supported or tolerated by the Christian faith, and he made a decision to stand against them. Contemporary Christian leaders face their own Bonhoeffer moments. It may be in regard to personal matters, such as telling the truth in conversations, or in regard to behind-the-scenes conduct—what we read, watch, and think. It is easy to compromise in small ways that don't seem to matter, but indeed they do, because small things are indicative of character. If a leader does not stand against the small evils, he or she is less likely to do so in the big moments.

Your Bonhoeffer moment may come on a more public scale. Bonhoeffer said that authentic Christianity protects the oppressed from the oppressor. Christianity without this kind of discipleship is Christianity without Christ. In our day, evil has been airbrushed and we have become desensitized to it, so we let it go. The most obvious evil in our day is abortion; Christians must continue to stand against it in word and deeds. Individuals need to speak against it, but so do churches and citizen organizations. The state continues to encroach on religious liberty, and it does so in the name of compassion and human rights. Whether it is forcing the church to pay for contraceptives or limiting a pastor's freedom to preach his conscience, beware of evil dressed up as kindness.

The church is also selling out its primary mission of being and making disciples. This evil is less obvious and its results are not easily noticed because of the rare but noticeable success of large churches. It is not that the larger churches are the problem themselves; it is that they distract the easily impressed, unstudied mind of the Christian world. The sad result is that discipleship is overlooked and Christians become compromised in their convictions. And all of us know, of course, that compromised character compromises.

Of all the leaders in America, the most important are pastors.

They are the last group of cultural teachers that remain a force for good. They are not strapped with limitations of government; they still have the freedom to teach and to act without restraint. For these three hundred thousand men and women in this country, this is a Bonhoeffer moment. It is time to step up and speak out, to commit their lives and people to a life of discipleship. For as Bonhoeffer said himself, "When Christ calls a man, he bids him to come and die." That is sacrificial leadership.

# The Rewards
# of Leadership

## REHABILITATE WHAT
## YOU WANT OUT OF IT

Therefore God exalted him to the
highest place and gave him the
name that is above every name.

**Philippians 2:9**

I want to thank all the little people.

**J. R. R. Tolkien**

**WHEN JAMES AND JOHN ASKED** for VIP seats in heaven, Jesus told them that he was not in charge of eternal seating. By now, two thousand years later, I suspect that all the special seats in heaven are sold out. All the VIP seats have been taken by apostles, prophets, and televangelists. There is, however, a way we all get to slip in — the ultimate "hole-in-the-wall gang." The joke is on the celestial muckety-mucks. We are all going to be seated in heaven with Christ. Paul explains, "God raised us up with Christ and seated us with him in the heavenly realms in Christ Jesus."[1]

I hope we don't have assigned seats in heaven so that we can wander around a bit and enjoy the place. Heaven holds rewards and possibly special perks for leaders. Will there be a "green room" for all the celebrities, authors, singers, actors, megachurch pastors, denominational executives, and Christian agents who wrote all the bonuses into their clients' contracts? Heaven will be heaven because someone in charge will tell the once-famous, "You will need to get that yourself." No valets in heaven.

So much for speculation. I don't want to talk about heavenly rewards as much as the rewards of leadership right now. What do you want to get out of being a leader?

## You Can Be Recognized and Rewarded Now

I believe in life after death, but I also believe in life *before* death. Jesus declared, "The thief comes only to steal and kill and destroy; I have come that they may have life, and have it to the full."[2]

A major part of human development is recognition. I don't

want to go too far back into my inner child—I will leave that to the psychologists—but I can remember being awarded a cute little New Testament for six months' perfect attendance at Northside Pilgrim Holiness Church in Indianapolis. This proves that my family didn't go anywhere on weekends. We never went anywhere period. (Maybe that is the reason I have been everywhere.)

The most nervous I have ever been was at the Indianapolis Public Library in 1955, when at age nine I played my first piano recital. Dressed in my white shirt and blue bow tie, I sat down at the piano and played "Sleigh Bells" in the key of C from John Thompson's first-grade book. There was polite applause. I took a bow, mission accomplished. I could have been a concert pianist, but alas, both my pinkies are crooked.

We all know that accomplishments and recognition build confidence. Fortunate children are surrounded with affirmation. Most of the adults in my life rewarded me when I did well. In those days, kids weren't burdened with a trophy for finishing ninth in a race or for just showing up. Awards were given to those who distinguished themselves. I found some affirmation in sports, especially basketball. At age thirteen, I played my first organized game in a run-down gym with a tile floor and scored fourteen points. Coaches, other players, and—most important to me—cute girls suddenly liked me. People wanted to hang out with me. Most of the time this recognition led to good conduct, but as we know, success can foster bad stuff too.

## Rewards Come with Risks

Being a successful Christian leader comes with risks. Well-meaning people admire, recognize, reward, praise, and lavish material goods on you. You begin to feel invincible. If you are not careful, you can forget where you are—that you are standing on

The Rewards of Leadership

the pinnacle of the temple with a voice whispering in your ear, "Jump. Go ahead! You can fly." And if you do jump, for a time you may fly, but when you begin to fall, you will remember that you have no wings.

The risk of success not only involves the unholy trinity of money, sex, and power; it also includes the danger of living a religious life with no power. There is nothing quite so odious. Jesus taught that being open and honest were keys to knowing God.[3] Religion, however, tends to make people closed and dishonest.[4] The Pharisees were religious but had no power. Jesus wasn't religious, but he had all the power. Jesus had no political power; the Pharisees had nothing but political power. Jesus scolded them for hypocrisy.[5]

Fame can ruin you, for it can cause you to be full of yourself. It happens to actors, singers, painters, poets, CEOs, pastors, athletes, and even to kids who just got an A on a test. We see this in sports today. When I was a basketball player in the 1960s and 1970s, taunting the other team with our success was nonexistent. We didn't talk smack and we certainly didn't point at opponents after scoring — especially when our team was down by twenty points! This kind of behavior is all part of a deconstructed culture that has changed from one of humility in achievement to arrogance in all things.

Many Christian leaders have faced the risks that come with fame and have not succumbed. One thinks first of Billy Graham, who has lived humbly and has been admired for his compassion, conviction, and authenticity. Rick Warren is another who has done well with fame. When it became public that he had paid back the salary he'd received from his church over the years and given away 90 percent of his book royalties, he silenced all sane critics. I think too of the great British pastor, John Stott. He lived a frugal and celibate life and was a wonderful example to his international flock. He wrote some of the best and most important books of our time, including commentaries on Romans and Galatians, *Basic Christianity*, and *Between Two Worlds*. Graham, Warren, and Stott exemplified the advice given by Mo Udall, the congressman "too funny to be president." When Udall was asked about the dangers of the intoxicating air of power in the halls of Congress, he answered, "The trick is not to inhale."[6]

It is too bad that inhaling fame doesn't have the same effect as when you first inhale a cigarette. When you hack and cough and get sick, your body is trying to tell you something. Fame is like an addictive drug that gives you a serious high and leaves you craving more. It's a powerful thing to have people "eating out of your hand." You can get that sense when you propose a course of action and everyone signs on. It happens to public speakers when people are caught in the sway of their talent and words. Before you know it, you drop your guard and take a big drag. Oh, the sweet smell of success.

I recently met a young evangelical pastor who is enjoying success and God's favor. He is well educated, hip, and a bit Bohemian. His congregation is young and the church services are full of energy, wonderful worship, dynamic preaching, and vivacious, enthusiastic leadership. The pastor is humble, teachable, and committed to authentic worship and discipleship. The congregation is with him and willing to follow him. Each week they pray for another church or ministry in the city. The Sunday I was there they prayed for a local Catholic church. People in the church speak of living and working outside the four walls of the church. These Christians are doing what Bonhoeffer meant when he said the church is the church only when it exists for others. This young leader is standing on the pinnacle of the temple. He is on a very high place. Satan is telling him to jump. God is telling him to walk humbly before him. We pray that he will continue to resist the temptation to try to fly on his own.

# The Reward of Witnessing Progress in Others

In this section I want to circle back around to the theme of chapter 2, "What Makes a Leader Happy?" The greatest reward a leader can experience in this life is the joy of seeing progress in others. "For what is our hope, our joy, or the crown in which we will glory in the presence of our Lord Jesus when he comes? Is it not you? Indeed, you are our glory and joy," Paul assured the Christians in Thessalonica.[7]

Archie Manning feels this kind of joy. He was an All-American quarterback at the University of Mississippi and a two-time Pro Bowl selection while with the New Orleans Saints. Archie has received great honor in his career, but nothing compares to what he feels watching his sons Peyton and Eli. Not only are both men great NFL quarterbacks who have won Super Bowls and been named MVPs, but they are also good men. That is as good as it gets. I would think that Archie feels the same way about his oldest son, Cooper, who was injured and never reached such athletic heights. There is great reward in seeing both your protégés and your progeny doing well.

## As a Teacher

In his memoir, Eugene Peterson wrote:

As I reflect with you on my fifty years in this pastoral vocation, it strikes me right now as curious that I have almost no sense of achievement. Doesn't that seem odd? What I remember is all the little detours into "proud" and "astray" that I experienced, the near misses, the staggering recoveries or semirecoveries of who I was and what I was about. People who look at me now have no idea how precarious it felt at the time, how many faithless stretches there were.[8]

In other words, Peterson wondered, "Why would anyone listen to me?" I can relate. When I sit across the table from a younger man, I often think, *If you only knew how much I don't know.* Progress is our goal, not perfection. Paul told his protégé, Timothy, "Be diligent in these matters; give yourself wholly to them, so that everyone may see your progress."[9]

My greatest satisfaction has always been that others have caught the same vision for life as I have. I recall early mornings with Ron, Gary, Cliff, and Doug. We saw ourselves as a team called to lead our congregation. Then, because of our efforts, others who became the core of our leadership joined us. When they began to lead and the church saw their commitment, my heart was full and satisfied. As all of us are now in our sixties, we can look back with satisfaction at what God did then and what he continues to do now, as some of these men are on my board of directors.

I gave some of my best sermons to a handful of men at 5:30 a.m. on Tuesdays with a cup of coffee in one hand and a doughnut in the other. I would use conflicts in the church as teachable moments. I would rant and rave about silly people and why they were silly. Most of all, I taught why the life of a disciple of Christ is the most satisfying and important life that can be lived. I was rewarded when I saw these men changing as they led others.

For example, our junior high pastor came up with the idea of Heavenly House, an alternative to the haunted house attraction in our town. The idea was to use our church's Christian education building as an indoor promenade, where people could walk from room to room to view various Bible scenes: Pentecost, Jesus' healing of the demoniac, Moses leading the children of Israel across the Red Sea, and so on. This required over a hundred workers, a good deal of funds, and a remodel of the Christian education house. The church trustees, however, had no vision for the project and felt it was a waste of money.

But I disagreed and made sure Heavenly House happened. Many people were angry with me. The first night, we hired a Christian rock band to play in the parking lot, and we provided refreshments for those waiting in line. We were shocked when thousands showed up and stood in long lines to go through the display. All three local television networks came and covered the story for the evening news.

I was standing in the parking lot, enjoying every minute, when I saw a group of grumpy guys complaining and talking about closing Heavenly House down because of the uproar it had created. "This can't be of God. People are having too much fun. Look at the mess they are making," some groused. Several of the younger men I had been working with walked up and joined in the conversation. After listening for a few minutes, one of my guys said, "I'll tell you what. If all of you will resign your leadership positions, we will see to it that you will be replaced. Because we don't want to hear all this negativity. We're finished with it." I must confess I was flooded with pleasure; it shot through my body and gave me a pastoral high. When you see those you lead rail against the religiosity that has caused so many to turn away from Christ, it is a wonderful day. This is the kind of reward I live for.

Recently, I have found great joy in working with a number of businessmen. One man who stands out is Steve, an attorney, who attended a lecture series I was doing on my book *Christlike*.[10] He and some others decided to join me in a two-year discipleship community. After a month, Steve started asking himself, "If Jesus were an attorney, what kind of attorney would he be?" It occurred to Steve that he could pray for his client, the judge, the jury, and even the opposing attorney while sitting in the courtroom. This was the first of many insights Steve had about how to act like Christ in the secular community. In fact, he has started a study group with people at his office who want to enroll in *Choose the*

*Life Journey*.[11] I am thrilled and I have his back as he begins to lead others. Another group of men in Newport Beach have now done the same; they are leading groups with the *Choose the Life* material. Nothing makes me happier than to be with these men and behold the dramatic changes in their lives, and to have their wives confirm those changes.

## As a Writer to Pastors

For most of my life, I have lived in a pastoral world. I have been a pastor, written for pastors, and helped pastors more than any other group. Even though all pastors feel a bit odd about being pastors, it is our life. We can't figure out how to do anything else. We are not better people than the average person; we just have been tapped on the shoulder by God to do this work.

My greatest rewards come from the pastors I have helped. It is quite satisfying to receive a thank-you for my ministry or to be quoted. Many pastors have talked with me about how much my written work has guided their lives. Sometimes it is frightening to know how much influence I have had on thousands of pastors and parishioners around the globe. When my plane lifts off the ground from yet another city where I have ministered, I often get a rush of thanksgiving. I have done well; I have helped someone, and I have left behind ideas and books. There are great rewards in being noticed, wanted, and respected. They are much better than trophies.

Making a difference is what motivates me to keep writing, sitting down daily and putting my feet under the desk and typing words up on the screen. The goal of my instruction has been to convince leaders to invest their lives in teaching others to obey everything that Christ commanded. I have always believed that there is nothing wrong with the church that discipleship cannot cure. Discipleship is the hope of the world because it produces a quality of life that preserves the moral character of a society and illuminates the darkest corners of the human personality.

Dallas Willard wrote, "It will come as a shock to many to think that Jesus did not tell his followers to make Christians or start churches, as we automatically think of Christians and churches today."[12] My bottom-line message to pastors is this: Jesus told us to make disciples, and if we commit to that, all other subsidiary activities such as conversion and church planting will take care of themselves. They are by-products, not the product themselves.

# Doing Things the Jesus Way

There is a deep satisfaction in knowing you have not exploited people in order to help them, knowing that what you have accomplished has been done the Jesus way. Eugene Peterson wrote:

> The ways Jesus goes about loving and saving the world are personal: nothing disembodied, nothing abstract, nothing impersonal. Incarnate, flesh and blood, relational, particular, local.[13]

Peterson went on to share his concern that ministry in North America is "conspicuously impersonal: programs, organizations," and that a "vocabulary of numbers is preferred over names." He sharpened his point by saying, "This is wrong thinking, and wrong living. Jesus is an alternative to the dominant ways of the world, not a supplement to them. We cannot use impersonal means to do or say a personal thing—and the gospel is personal or it is nothing."[14]

Earlier I mentioned hearing Dallas Willard say he was committed to not trying to make things happen. Dallas wanted to do things the Jesus way. He didn't want to accomplish something unless it was done at God's prompting. Leaders who start things may find this particularly challenging. How do you know that what you started was truly from God's prompting? If you started your ministry or church the same way you might start a business, you are likely following a secular model rather than the Jesus model of leadership. Let me explain this.

A business model for starting something takes the following approach. You develop a plan and come up with a logo, a motto, a look, and a brand. Then you purchase names from a marketing firm and send out announcements to possible customers. Then you follow up with phone calls from a team of paid callers who survey preferences from the community. You offer prizes or incentives to those who attend the meetings. You continue to survey them to make sure you are giving your customers what they want. If you are starting a church, you preach about how the gospel helps people develop a better life, how it will enhance everything from their families to their winning personalities.

This, Peterson would say, is the American way, which is stubbornly resistant to the way of Jesus. The contemporary church is designed to meet the perceived needs of both clergy and congregation. Pastors "need" their churches to grow so that they can make a living and feel successful. Their congregations "need" their churches to meet their needs of self-actualization. They want to go to a church where they like the music, preaching, and youth ministry. They want church to cater to their likes and dislikes as a consumer. Consequently, the American church is customized to serve the people. This is significantly distinct from the idea that the purpose of the church is to teach people that they are to serve and live for others.

The Jesus way to start a ministry or church begins with prayer. You act only when the Spirit of God moves you to act. At the same time, your plan is to teach people what Scripture says they need to become. You don't view people as a means to your end as a leader. If we approach decision making the Jesus way, I don't think we will be plagued with doubts about whether we are making the right decision. I've learned this the hard way.

After graduation from seminary, I was bored with my church and looking for a challenge. The conventional wisdom then was that a bigger church would be a better church. The Jesus way to approach this decision would have been to pray about my future and tell no one about what I was thinking. But I was impatient. I couldn't wait that long, so I put my name out and asked around if there were any openings in the denomination. I began to receive letters. I read over the options and filled out and returned a few of the forms. Over time, I interviewed with a few churches, and one invited me to become its nominated choice to be pastor. After a few days of getting to know me, they offered me the position, which I accepted. God used me greatly in that church, and while there I wrote my first book. But I must admit that I am not sure whether God sent me there or whether he made the best out of my impatience and lack of trust.

Am I saying that Christians shouldn't send out résumés or use placement services to get jobs? This is treacherous territory because many good and godly men and women have done so. But the Jesus way does seem to me to be a superior way to live. It does not lead to passivity; it leads to a deeper and a more committed way to live where you are now. It requires us to abandon self-promotion. Over the last decade I have gradually moved from the promoted life to the received life. In the past ten years I have not asked to speak anywhere or sent out a résumé. I have followed the motto that if you do good work, people will notice. Even so, I continue to struggle with my level of aggressiveness in attempting to influence others.

Faith's primary property is action, and the action we take matters. I have looked at my calendar in the past and have seen three months of blank space, meaning I had no speaking engagements. I know that I have a great and positive impact when I do speak, but what is God saying to me when I have three months of no speaking engagements? When I approach this situation the Jesus way, my first action is to pray for peace and contentment, and the second is to live out the axiom, "Seek not to speak — seek to have something to say." Then I pray that God will lead people to invite me to speak at events that will advance the message of disciple making and discipleship around the world. Without exception, when I do this, my schedule fills up in wonderful and unexpected ways. I also begin to realize that there are others who can bring this message, and that I don't have the right but the privilege to speak.

If I am not being asked to speak for a time, it doesn't mean God doesn't value my life's work or opinion. It means I should prepare, like the harpooner in *Moby-Dick*, to sit quietly until it is time to stand and strike. It could be that the speaking engagement that God has assigned to me is to incarnate the Word of God in my friendship and conversation with my neighbors because there is no other person to fill that slot but me. Oftentimes the largest leap of faith for leaders is to think of their ordinary lives as being as important as their public lives.

Three years ago I was awakened in the wee hours of the morning. It was one of those rare moments when God spoke clearly to me. I had been asking him, "How can I make best use of my knowledge and skills for you in this fourth quarter of life?" The plan rolled out for me in a way so clear and simple that it frightened me, leading to the creation of a new ministry called The Bonhoeffer Project. This is a process that takes leaders and teaches them to be disciple makers. I understood that God had given me permission to initiate, create, and be more aggressive in pursuing this vision, and that is an amazing gift, a reward.

We now turn to how God rewards us and how we handle those rewards.

# Heaven's Reward System

A dear friend of mine, Dr. Terry Dischinger, was a three-time first-team All-American basketball player at Purdue University. He played on the 1960 Olympic basketball team and was a great player in the NBA for several years. He also is a member of the Basketball Hall of Fame. No honorable-mention life for Terry.

The same can't be said of me. I received honorable-mention kudos as a junior college All-American. When I was featured in *Sports Illustrated* dunking the ball, I was standing on a ladder. Honorable mention pretty much describes my life: good enough, but not quite the best. I have operated mostly under the radar. I have been working on my honorary doctorate for years; it has yet to come. I have had agents and publicists who tried to put me on top, but fame keeps giving me the slip. I have learned to live on the second tier. I speak at a few big events, but mostly I get the gig in January at the Saskatchewan Bigfoot Bible Institute Pastors' Conference.

If we wait for our fellow workers and colleagues to affirm us, we may not get enough affirmation to sustain us. After a while, a person just gets tired of competing. Some think that we feel contentment in our mature years because we have learned to be content in whatever circumstances we find ourselves. My wife has assured me, however, that my contentment comes from a reduction in testosterone. If I took a shot of testosterone, she says, I would lace up my old sneakers and get after it.

Jesus departed this world as a hero with only about five hundred witnesses to his resurrection. The important people in charge of Israel said, "Good riddance." But Jesus had a different view. He was returning to his Father; he was preparing a place for his followers. He was going to sit at his Father's right hand and plead our case, hear our prayers, and send the Holy Spirit to remind his followers of everything he taught. His Father also had a different view because he elevated Jesus to the highest place of honor and gave him a name above all names.

Heaven has its own reward system. Quite often the actual reward is delayed, as in the case of Jesus. Jesus has yet to have his day or get his due. He hasn't ridden in on his white horse yet, every knee has yet to bow, and every tongue has not yet confessed that he is Lord. The world system and many of its inhabitants continue to ridicule him or consider him irrelevant. Yet Jesus waits. He patiently goes about his business of keeping his church afloat, of sustaining his people, of holding their hands and fulfilling his promise to be with them until the end.

The whole idea of Jesus' vindication comes up at this point. In the rewards game it seems as though Jesus finally does get his due, as everyone who has ever lived will acknowledge his authority. Is that a reward for Jesus? Does Jesus really need it? He does deserve it, but does he require it for his own pleasure? Is it the biggest "I told you so" moment in human history? This seems a bit vindictive. After the ceremony, do we shuffle the once-skeptical unbeliever to the bus to hell? I point this out because if my expectation of reward is vindication, then likely I have it wrong. My hunch is that for heaven to be heaven, it will not indulge the lower nature with its desire to be great and right and vindicated in all the worst ways. If vindication is the reward I am looking for, I will be disappointed.

The apostle Paul visited the third heaven, otherwise known as the abode of God.[15] Let's let him be our guide to our heavenly rewards:

> For I am already being poured out like a drink offering, and the time for my departure is near. I have fought the good fight, I have finished the race, I have kept the faith. Now there is in store for me the crown of righteousness, which the Lord, the righteous Judge, will award to me on that

day — and not only to me, but also to all who have longed
for his appearing.[16]

I have never been crowned, but it must be an intoxicating experience. I expect that most of us will get crowns of righteousness, and
we might wear them only for special occasions. I also think that
all this talk about literal crowns could be symbolic. Perhaps God is
simply giving us an earthly image of a beyond-our-comprehension,
divine reality. Regardless, the passage above confirms that that we
will be rewarded. If we obey and teach Christ's commands, we will
be called great in heaven.[17]

In the end the rewards that satisfy are simple.

One of my great memories is of the day I received news that my
first book, *Jesus Christ, Disciplemaker*, would be published. It was
a moment of pristine joy, the pleasure of knowing that God had
rewarded my desire to speak for him. It reminded me of William
Blake's words:

> He who binds to himself a joy
> Does the winged life destroy;
> But he who kisses the joy as it flies
> Lives in Eternity's sun rise.[18]

On this side of the heavenly divide we often receive our recognition with pride. In heaven it will be with humility. We will be
inclined to share the crown, to think of ourselves as undeserving.
The rewards God gives will survive the fire of his judgment and
discerning eye.[19] When our letters, trophies, and mementos are lost
or destroyed, what God has called great and good will remain with
us forever.

# Leaders Are a Work in Progress

## REHABILITATE YOUR HEART TO STAY IN THE STRUGGLE

> For it is God who works in you to will and to act in order to fulfill his good purpose.
>
> **Philippians 2:13**

> I read in a periodical the other day that the fundamental thing is how we think about God. By God Himself, it is not! How God thinks of us is not only more important, but infinitely more important.
>
> **C. S. Lewis, *The Weight of Glory***

**LEADERS ARE** a work in progress. Isn't this obvious? It takes a lifetime to learn just a little about pleasing God. That is why we don't retire from the school of discipleship. That is why we don't ever arrive or learn enough. We can't kick back and coast once we acquire a certain level of knowledge and maturity. People of a certain age often find it easy to coast, to live on yesterday's manna and drop out from the struggle of inner change. But when we do, our heart for God withers away. There is a better way.

A. W. Tozer famously said in *The Knowledge of the Holy*, "What comes into our minds when we think about God is the most important thing about us."[1] I understand Tozer's meaning and would not dispute its importance. But I would challenge the idea that what I think about God is the single most important thing about me. I must cast my lot with C. S. Lewis who said in his famous sermon *The Weight of Glory*, "I read in a periodical the other day that the fundamental thing is how we think about God. By God Himself, it is not! How God thinks of us is not only more important, but infinitely more important."[2]

Indeed, how we think of God is of no importance except as it is related to how he thinks of us. God thinks of me as his masterpiece. Paul affirmed, "For we are God's masterpiece. He has created us anew in Christ Jesus, so we can do the good things he planned for us long ago."[3] A masterpiece is a signature work of art. It is the best work of a skilled artisan. For example, Margaret Mitchell's *Gone with the Wind* and Harper Lee's *To Kill a Mockingbird* are their author's singular great works. We are the crown of creation; we are what God has done best. We are the centerpieces of his work. The author of Hebrews spoke to this. What is mankind that you are mindful of them, a son of man that you care for him? You made them a little lower than the angels; you crowned them with glory and honor and put everything under their feet."[4]

God continues to work with me, not on me, for all of my days. His purpose is that I become like him. As the apostle Paul put it:

> Do everything without grumbling or arguing, so that you may become blameless and pure, "children of God without fault in a warped and crooked generation." Then you will shine among them like stars in the sky as you hold firmly to the word of life. And then I will be able to boast on the day of Christ that I did not run or labor in vain.[5]

I like how Lewis described what God has in mind for us:

> Imagine yourself as a living house. God comes in to rebuild that house. At first, perhaps, you can understand what He is doing. He is getting the drains right and stopping the leaks in the roof and so on: you knew that those jobs needed doing and so you are not surprised. But presently he starts knocking the house about in a way that hurts abominably and does not seem to make sense. What on earth is He up to? The explanation is that He is building quite a different house from the one you thought of — throwing out a new wing here, putting on an extra floor there, running up towers, making courtyards. You thought you were going to be made into a decent little cottage: but He is building a palace. He intends to come and live in it Himself.[6]

I just spoke with a friend whose recent church experience illustrates what this looks like in real life. After he had been at the church for nine years, his contract as pastor was not renewed. Apparently, his denomination calls a pastor for a term and then evaluates his ministry. A board composed of people whom he had loved and helped dismissed him. The story goes much deeper and of course there are always two sides. My friend arrived at the church when it was in crisis. It had gone through a horrendous split and people were hurt and angry. He was an experienced man, a gifted man, but new to the pastoral life. He mistakenly thought he could treat Christians in churches like normal people. He didn't realize that Christians check their normal heads at the door to the church and screw on their zany "Christian heads." There he was, a church-environment acolyte in the middle of hurt, anger, and vulnerable followers of Jesus. He made a few mistakes and it cost him. During his first three years, most of those who were bound to leave did, and a new crop of people came in. I met him during this time and he committed himself to a life of discipleship and to help his congregants learn what it means to be apprentices of Jesus.

The nine years at this church were a crucible. It never got easy. Many of the congregants didn't change, but the good news is that my friend changed greatly. This pastor and his family loved and loved even more; they loved even when they were out of love. It was unfair of the board to treat him this way, but what a gift the situation has been to my friend, his wife, and their children! He refused to fight. He committed to going deeper with God, to becoming gracious, kind, loving, and forgiving. That church will probably never find a better man to lead them again. So few would "hug the cactus" that long.

But as C. S. Lewis said, "You thought you were going to be made into a decent little cottage: but He is building a palace. He intends to come and live in it Himself." My friend walked into that church as a cottage under construction, and he walked out with his head held high, as a palace fit for his King. Years from now, people will say of him, "We didn't know what we had in him." They will lament how he was treated and recognize how Christlike he behaved; they will not see his like again. They wanted a bigger church. They wanted to be noticed and respected for being a great church in the way that the secular world names greatness. His legacy was not a bigger church, but the "bigger" Christians he left behind.

I want to present the basic thought of this chapter in one verse: "It is God who works in you to will and to act in order to fulfill his good purpose."[7] It tells the story of how we learn. Learning as a disciple, an apprentice of Jesus, is a supernatural process. It touches the deepest part of our souls for all our lives.

## "For It Is God Who Works in You"

Christian leadership calls for authentic living. It requires humility, service, vulnerability, sacrificial living, and the willingness to put up with a constant stream of abuse. Sometimes that abuse and criticism can be mere street noise, but other times it is a jackhammer in your head. The Christian leader is called to receive criticism in humility, to learn from it, to admit one's faults, and to not seek revenge. An argument can be made that any sensible person would not choose to be a Christian leader.

I wrote earlier that a role in leadership first came to me in east Africa in 1968 when I delivered a sermon to sixty-five villagers. I must ask, who made the choice for me to be a leader? Who chooses whom for Christian leadership? I find it interesting that when Samuel went to check out Jesse's sons to find a king for Israel, David wasn't even there. He was out minding his flock, taking care of business without a kingly thought. After looking over all of David's brothers, Samuel knew he had yet to meet the right one. When Samuel selected him to be the next king, David was the most surprised of all of them. I felt the same about God's call on my life to preach. I was swept away with it all. The very next day I preached in a bus station in downtown Nairobi. I was kneeling with several men on a sidewalk, praying with them. It was surreal. I had never envisioned this for my life. And yet, looking back, I can see God at work all along the way. Of all the schools I could have chosen to play for after my two years in junior college, I chose Oral Roberts University. Two months after arriving on campus, I slipped out of my bed onto my knees and committed my life to Christ.

I think of those nights in the men's dorm in northeastern Oklahoma when, after a Saturday night of doing all the things my grandmother prayed against, I would think about the flames of hell. I knew I was headed there, but in the back of my mind I thought, *Someday I will right the ship.* On Sunday mornings, a faithful Baptist pastor would rap on my window until my roommate would curse him and he would go away. He was there because I couldn't tell him to his face that I wouldn't go to church with him. He came Sunday after Sunday; I never went.

I did a lot of risky things my first two years in college, but something restrained me, kept me from doing things that would cost me down the line. I vividly remember telling a girl that I could no longer date her. She was so angry she screamed at me, and I hid in my dorm room while she called me every name in the book. As I lay there listening to her screaming from outside my window, I kept thinking, *I can't keep this up. My grandparents, my mother — I can't disgrace them.* My grandmother's prayers were at work in me; God was at work in me.

I have often reflected on the fact that nowhere in the New Testament did God call anyone to leadership as a paid religious professional. I can't say God's call to me was to be a pastor or to work for a mission enterprise. It was a call to organize my life around his purpose for my life. I have intentionally never tried to figure out the calling. The conceit of the mind can destroy life's sweetest truth that God knows me and has told me what to do. What Tolstoy wrote of science applies: "Science is meaningless because it gives no answer to our question, the only question important to us, 'what shall we do and how shall we live?'"[8]

I first thought of Christian leadership as preaching, which makes sense because that is the only Christian leadership I had ever exercised. When I returned home from Africa for my senior year of college, I noticed a difference in my thinking and in how others treated me. People began to see me as a leader. I was chosen co-captain of the basketball team. In my senior year, I was awarded the President's Cup, an honor given to the student athlete who most exemplified the goals of the university. More importantly, I began to think of myself as a leader with the call of Christ on my life. I announced to my fiancée, Jane, that I had been "called." She had vowed never to marry a medical doctor or a minister. It was too late; she was swept up in the call with me. I continued to be blessed as a basketball player and had a great year, but the overarching reality in my life was the growing desire to serve Christ.

God was working in me to give me a confidence that was based not on my own experience but upon his call. He used my athletic training to make me fearless regarding what he and others asked of me.

## "To Will and to Act"

My first year out of college, I joined the Athletes in Action basketball team because more than playing basketball, I wanted to do mission work. The NBA did not draft me, but even if it had, it wouldn't have mattered. Some of the players dreamed of going professional; it never crossed my mind, even when I was the leading scorer after my rookie year. I wanted to speak for Christ. I had lost interest in basketball as my primary passion.

Whenever our team played a team like North Carolina, we spent three days on campus speaking to fraternities, to local civic groups, and at Campus Crusade for Christ student events. As a rookie, I not only had to earn my playing time, I had to earn my speaking time as well. I began to tell the coach that I was called to preach and that if I couldn't speak more I would not return the next year; I would become a pastor. The coach, who later became a psychologist, told me that I was too inexperienced to be a pastor and didn't know the Bible well enough. He was right, of course, but the conversation revealed my passion: God had given me the desire to lead. Scripture tells us that the desire to lead in the church is a good thing.[9] Without such a desire, Christian leadership is a nonstarter. If a gifted person has no desire to lead, then that should be enough to convince everyone that God did not call that person to lead. We are told, "For it is God who *works in you to will* and to act in order to fulfill his good purpose."[10] God works his will in our will, and then he goes to work to make it happen.

God worked his will in me during the summer of 1967. I had accepted the basketball scholarship to Oral Roberts University and gone home to Indianapolis for the summer to work and prepare for my move to ORU. My friends in Indianapolis were not Christian, and I certainly was not. They pressured me to go to a different university. Maury John, the legendary coach at Drake University, had also recruited me. At that time, Drake had a nationally ranked team and played in arguably the nation's toughest basketball conference, the Missouri Valley. I started thinking, *Why waste my talent at ORU when I could go to Drake?* I contacted Coach John, signed a national letter of intent, and enrolled at Drake. Now I had my Drake jacket and all the prestige that went with it. I also decided to eat as much pizza and drink as much beer as I could that summer and started to gain some weight. I was in a discipline-free zone, absent of any structure.

In August, my junior-college coach, Cletus Green, and the Oral Roberts coach, Bill White, decided to visit me in Indianapolis. I knew they had come to talk me into switching back to ORU. They treated me to a juicy steak dinner, and then it was off to a

Holiday Inn for the interrogation. At some point in the conversation they brought up my old girlfriend, Jeannie, Johnnie, Jonie, Janie — whatever her name was. They wanted to know if she would like to go to ORU. I kept my composure. Janie and I had not dated in months, but we had agreed to write to each other over the summer. She was planning to attend Kansas State Teachers College in Emporia, and I was going to Drake in Des Moines. Not much of a future. For some reason that I didn't understand then, I acted as if we were an item and said, "I don't know. If I change my mind, I will give her a call." Over the next few days, I pondered what to do. I finally called Janie to see what she said. I was sure she would say she had no interest in going to ORU, but she said she would go there if I was going there. School began in thirty days. If she was willing to go to ORU, obviously, I had to go as well. Thirty days later Janie and I stood hand in hand on the ORU campus, both thinking, *What in the world have we done?*

God was at work "to will" in me, to get me off my desires and onto his. He used my junior-college coach, Janie, and even her mother. You see, Janie didn't really make up her mind to go to ORU until she and her mother reached a literal fork in the road, north to Kansas or south to Tulsa, and her mother said, "Let's go to ORU." Yes, my friends, God even uses future mothers-in-law to get it done.

## Unchecked Desire

We live in a society dominated by desire. Our culture encourages us to act on desire and to let the various lusts of life direct us. We don't always recognize our evil desires for what they are. We tell ourselves we're being just a bit naughty or that we are blowing off a little steam. But Scripture tells us to put to death the desires of the flesh, especially those that lead to anger, malice, slander, and obscene talk and experience.[11] Desire out of the context of God's will is dangerous.

I think of the late film producer and impresario Jerry Weintraub, who is portrayed in the HBO documentary *His Way* as a lusty deal-maker who never takes no for an answer. The stories of his woman-izing and making deals are funny but tragic. He is a man run by desire. John Calvin put it well: "The ruin of a man is to obey himself."

Money and sex are hot, garish sins made for the media. But we must turn our attention to something much subtler. It is the desire that whispers deeply in the Christian leader's soul. It is the desire to win, to take up arms to make yourself look good, to have the last word.

# The Desire to Be Vindicated

We see this subtle desire in King David at the end of his life when he gave instructions to his son Solomon, who was soon to take the throne. David began by saying all the right things about obedience to God and keeping his law. And then he said:

> Now you yourself know what Joab son of Zeruiah did to me — what he did to the two commanders of Israel's armies, Abner son of Ner and Amasa son of Jether. He killed them, shedding their blood in peacetime as if in battle, and with that blood he stained the belt around his waist and the san-dals on his feet. Deal with him according to your wisdom, but do not let his gray head go down to the grave in peace.... And remember, you have with you Shimei son of Gera, the Benjamite from Bahurim, who called down bitter curses on me... I swore to him by the LORD: "I will not put you to death by the sword." But now, do not consider him innocent. You are a man of wisdom; you will know what to do to him. Bring his gray head down to the grave in blood.[12]

Solomon was shrewd, and he took care of both men and a few others in a subtle and crafty way. But David's desire to win and to have revenge was evil and led to treachery and revenge. Whether you are a king in the middle of a battle or a leader dealing with people who oppose you in a church or business, how you respond to combative situations will reveal your character. Many years ago I found myself engaged in a battle for my reputation and my job. The situation tested my own desire, whether I was acting out of the desire for vindication or for God's purpose. As you read what happened, put yourself in my place and imagine how you might have conducted yourself.

I was a novice when it came to congregational intrigue; I had always been a straight shooter. The culture of this particular church reflected itself in broken relationships, suspicion, and vengeance. I remember one man in particular. At first he liked me, but as time passed, we disagreed on several issues, and he wanted me out. To this day, I am not sure what motivated him. He called my previous church and put together "facts" to prove I had lied about my experience there. He claimed that my previous congregation had fired me and that I had lied about how much I gave to the church financially. I was cleared of the accusations by a simple fact check.

He finally decided to write a letter to the president of our denomination and various superintendents, accusing me of a long list of violations. He did not copy me on the letter. He proceeded to follow Jane and me around the community. We would leave a restaurant and his car would be parked nearby. He would cruise by our house at odd hours; this was obvious since we lived on a cul-de-sac. Normally I would have confronted him one-on-one and had it out, but he would have distorted such action and used it against me. He held the confidence of many church members who believed he was representing their concerns.

I discussed at length with some of the staff and leaders how we might deal with this man's increasing anger and personal attacks on me. We came up with a way to address the problem. He held an important position in the church, and it was time for annual elections. His position was up for a vote. We asked him to vacate his position and run for another. He agreed, thinking that he would easily win the vote. We informed him that another person, a twenty-six-year-old novice, was running for the same position. This man didn't know how many people disliked his attacks on me. He was sure he would be elected, but we knew that many newer members and younger people would vote for the younger man. When the vote came back, he lost, the novice won, and our mission was accomplished. He was out. Later he was voted out of membership for continued actions.

There is no doubt that this man should have been removed because of his bitterness and his refusal to repent. But what about my friends and me? Were we in the clear for orchestrating his ouster? I won't speak about my friends, but I believe that I did the right thing in the wrong way. It was right to address the man's defiance, but I wanted vindication. I lowered myself and played the political game in order to win, to take out an enemy. I didn't love him and I didn't exactly treat him as Jesus treated Judas. I don't mean to say that he was on the level of Judas; my point is that Jesus treated Judas better than I treated this man. And for that I am sorry, of that I repent. My hope is that this man and I will embrace one day in heaven.

The need to win, to take up arms to make yourself look good or salvage your reputation, is a dangerous desire. Don't skim over this point. Take some time right now to analyze your actions when you've had to fight for your career or your reputation. What do your actions reveal about your character?

# "To Fulfill His Good Purpose"

Last Sunday right before our pastor was to preach, I leaned over and said to Jane, "I want to race the pastor to the pulpit and preach this sermon." The call to preach is permanent. It is wonderful how the work that pleases God also pleases the person called to do the work. When I pass a large church building, my pulse quickens. I may even salivate. The urge to preach, to lead, and to make it happen just won't go away. Jane says that I will end up in a skilled nursing facility full of preachers and we will just preach at each other all day. She thinks I will like it.

When God gives you a desire to do something, it doesn't diminish. The body and the mind may weaken, but you can't help fulfilling his call on your life until you can't do it anymore. Most Sundays I do not preach. I do a lot of speaking and communicating, but Sundays find me in the pew at my church. For the most part, this is because my pulpit has morphed into the written word. Most Sundays I am content to sit, but not always. I still struggle because I know I could be somewhere preaching.

Sunday mornings before church I lead a community of men and women who are committed to a life of discipleship. They are willing to live with accountability and to push themselves into new habits that will transform them into little Christs. Year after year I work with people like these and they are changed. They go on to lead others. I believe that I am accomplishing more by being in community with people than I would if I could preach at them for thirty minutes each week. Because when you live by covenant, you can't blow each other off. You must listen, trust, be humble, and live sacrificially. I think this accounts for my contentment in the pew. And it all stems from a desire and a power that God gave me on that windblown plain in east Africa in the summer of 1968, and I can't stop.

When it comes to pleasing God, I have had a lot to learn. The first twenty-one years of my life I thought what would make God happy would make me sad. I lived in a church world of women without makeup, jewelry, or uncut hair. Women, including little girls, wore long-sleeved dresses even on the hottest summer day. Boys were not allowed to wear shorts, which prevented them from playing most sports. Kids were not allowed to play on Sunday, see movies, watch television, or in general do all the things kids enjoy. I was taught that holiness was the deprivation of human pleasure and that the less pleasure a Christian had — the less we desired anything — the more God was pleased. I got out as soon as I could.

I no longer think that pleasure and desire are bad. In fact, I believe that most Christians suffer from a lack of desire. C. S. Lewis powerfully presented this idea:

> If you asked twenty good men today what they thought the highest of the virtues, nineteen of them would reply, Unselfishness. But if you asked almost any of the great Christians of old he would have replied, Love. You see what has happened? A negative term has been substituted for a positive, and this is of more than philological importance. The negative idea of Unselfishness carries with it the suggestion not primarily of securing good things for others, but of going without them ourselves, as if our abstinence and not their happiness was the important point.... Indeed, if we consider the unblushing promises of reward and the staggering nature of the rewards promised in the Gospels, it would seem that Our Lord finds our desires not too strong, but too weak. We are half-hearted creatures, fooling about with drink and sex and ambition when infinite joy is offered to us, like an ignorant child who wants to go on making mud pies in a slum because he cannot imagine what is meant by the offer of a holiday at the sea. We are far too easily pleased.[13]

In recent days my relationship to God has been especially joyous. Conditions are good and that helps. But I relish my days. They are full of—should I say it?—fun. I don't feel the weight of the world on my shoulders; I have given back the responsibility to change the world to God. He has relieved me of my self-importance. I can't stop leading, however; I step up and take over when I am needed. Daily I prod and probe people all over the globe through various forms of communication.

How wonderful it all is, "For it is God who works in you to will and to act in order to fulfill his good purpose."[14] God has given me contentment. I think of the apostle Paul when he was in prison and penned,

> I have learned to be content whatever the circumstances. I know what it is to be in need, and I know what it is to have plenty. I have learned the secret of being content in any and every situation, whether well fed or hungry, whether living in plenty or in want. I can do all this through him who gives me strength.[15]

I am happy doing work with others that does not grab the limelight. God has given me the desire to invest in people's lives and the power to govern my ego. These things please him and they please me.

God is pleased when we accept what he has made us to be. I spent much of my life trying to be someone else: the successful pastor, teacher, speaker, or leader. I was "wearing other people's faces," as May Sarton put it.[16] I resonate with what Parker Palmer wrote about himself and his work as a college president and teacher:

> Today I serve education from outside the institution where my pathology is less likely to get triggered—rather than from the inside, where I waste energy on anger instead of investing it in hope. This pathology, which took me years

to recognize, is my tendency to get so conflicted with the way people use power in institutions that I spend more time being angry at them than I spend on my real work. Once I understood that the problem was "in here" as well as "out there," the solution seemed clear: I needed to work independently, outside of institutions, detached from the stimuli that trigger my knee-jerk response. Having done just that for over a decade now, my pathology no longer troubles me: I have no one to blame but myself for whatever the trouble may be and am compelled to devote my energies to the work I am called to do![17]

It has been thirteen years since I left the world of organized religion. I attend meetings and work in ways that I never did as a pastor. I have found an interesting life on the other side of church life, the "I'm here just to be here and serve" side. I get a great deal of joy out of doing little things for God. I love to think about Francis Schaeffer's little volume *No Little People.*[18] I may now know what he meant. Jesus himself said, "He who is faithful in a very little is faithful also in much."[19] Can someone who was faithful in much learn to be faithful in little? I think so. Indeed, this leader is a work in progress.

# Notes

## Introduction

1. John Stott, *Basic Christian Leadership* (Downers Grove, IL: InterVarsity Press, 2002), 11.
2. The plan is commonly called the Great Commission. See Matthew 28:18–20 and Acts 1:5–8. It is not that the church has ignored these instructions; it's that we have at times misunderstood and misapplied them.
3. The church became a formally recognized religious entity within the Roman Empire with the Edict of Milan in 313 CE. This was both the apex of its success and the beginning of its decline. One hundred years later, it was compromised and corrupt.
4. Dallas Willard, *The Divine Conspiracy* (San Francisco: HarperSanFrancisco, 1998), 13.
5. Matthew 11:29–30.

## Chapter 1: The Rehabilitation of Christian Leaders

1. It needs to be said that science is not fixed knowledge. Its knowledge continues to grow, and new findings often disprove a previous theory. There is often little said, however, about the limits of scientific knowledge. Charles Darwin said that

189

scientific observation's purpose is to test a theory. Science is full of theories that are tested repeatedly, and by this method a certain knowledge is attained. Yet this kind of "truth" changes as the discipline develops over time. Religious knowledge is proved in a different way but can be just as true and more unchangeable. There are different ways of knowing and different kinds of knowledge.

2. See John 21:4–9.

3. Colossians 1:15–16.

4. Colossians 1:17.

5. See Colossians 1:19–20.

6. See Luke 2:41–52.

7. John 8:58–59.

8. John 14:9–10.

9. Matthew 16:15–17.

10. Rodney Stark, *Discovering God: The Origins of the Great Religions and the Evolution of Belief* (New York: HarperOne, 2007), 283–84.

11. See Matthew 28:20.

12. See Luke 24:35–43; John 21. He touched, cooked breakfast for, consumed food with, and coached and taught them, including giving special instructions to Peter (John 21:15–19). He breathed on them and filled them with the Holy Spirit (see John 20:22). In Luke 24:44–49 he taught them Scripture; he filled them with the Holy Spirit and told them they would be witnesses.

13. It should be acknowledged that the book of Acts presents a prophetic approach to evangelism that is direct, even confrontational. I do not want to eliminate this dimension from evangelism. It will always be needed, but relationships are the key to getting through. There is plenty of relational

evangelism in Acts, starting with 2:42–47, which emphasizes the power of community life and how it drew others to Christ.

14. David T. Olson, *The American Church in Crisis* (Grand Rapids: Zondervan, 2008).

15. "Six Megathemes from 2010," *Barna Group*, 13 December 2010, http://www.barna.org/barna-update/culture/462-six -megathemes-emerge-from-2010

16. "Six Megathemes," *Barna Group*.

17. "Six Megathemes," *Barna Group*.

18. Wesley's on-the-road schedule was to arrive at a village some-time before the evening meal and to preach that evening, then preach again very early before the workday the next morning. Wesley would then ride his horse to the next village or town and repeat the same process again, town after town. More can be learned by reading John Wesley's journal.

19. Dallas Willard, *In Search of Guidance* (San Francisco: HarperSanFrancisco, 1993), 227, 228.

20. Frederick Dale Bruner, *Matthew: The Christbook, Matthew 1–12* (Waco, TX: Word, 1987), 50, quoted in Eugene Peterson, *The Jesus Way: A Conversation on the Ways That Jesus Is the Way* (Grand Rapids: Eerdmans, 2007), 201.

21. I speak here of his ability to heal, raise the dead, demonstrate dominance over evil spirits, and know what people were thinking in that he read their minds. See John 2:22. See also his discourses in John 5:19–30 and 17:1–26 on how he and his Father worked together on what to do and when to do it.

22. See John 14:6.

23. Peterson, *The Jesus Way*, 2.

24. For a treatment of the importance of pastors as teachers to the nations, see Dallas Willard's *Knowing Christ Today*, chapter 8, "Pastors as Teachers of the Nations" (New York: HarperOne, 2009).

25. Dallas Willard, *The Spirit of the Disciplines* (San Francisco: Harper & Row, 1988), 246.
26. Andy Crouch, *Culture Making: Recovering Our Creative Calling* (Downers Grove, IL: InterVarsity Press, 2008), 188.
27. Rodney Stark, *God's Battalions* (San Francisco: HarperOne, 2009), 32.
28. Matthew 24:14.
29. Heaven as described in Revelation 21.

# Chapter 2: What Makes a Leader Happy?

1. Philippians 2:2.
2. Philippians 2:1 NLT.
3. See Matthew 28:18–20.
4. As cited in Malcolm Muggeridge, *A Third Testament* (Maryknoll, NY: Orbis, 2004), xiii.
5. Colossians 1:28–29 NLT.
6. Clayton M. Christensen, "How Will You Measure Your Life?" *Harvard Business Review*, July/August 2010, 46–51.
7. See Colossians 1:28–29; Galatians 4:19–20; Ephesians 4:11–17.
8. Christensen, "How Will You Measure Your Life?," 48.
9. Henri J. M. Nouwen, *In the Name of Jesus: Reflections on Christian Leadership* (New York: Crossroad, 1989).
10. Nouwen, *In the Name of Jesus*, 28.
11. Nouwen, *In the Name of Jesus*, 29–30, 43.
12. Nouwen, *In the Name of Jesus*, 77–79.
13. 1 Corinthians 11:1.
14. Philippians 3:3–4, 7–8 NLT.
15. Nouwen, *In the Name of Jesus*, 81–82.

# Chapter 3: Making a Dent in the World

1. Usually attributed to Steve Jobs, cofounder of Apple. See Walter Isaacson, *Steve Jobs: A Biography* (New York: Simon & Schuster, 2011), 94.
2. Colossians 1:29.
3. Galatians 4:19.
4. Letter to author from a friend. Used with permission.
5. See Philippians 2:3.
6. Eugene Peterson, *The Jesus Way: A Conversation on the Ways That Jesus Is the Way* (Grand Rapids: Eerdmans, 2007), 249.
7. Geoffrey Williamson, *The World of Josephus* (Baltimore: Penguin, 1959), 203.
8. This idea and line of thought about Josephus is found in Peterson, *The Jesus Way*, 243–51.
9. Ephesians 2:10 refers to "good works" that God prepared beforehand that we might walk in them. This is probably a general truth, but it has specific application in every life.
10. Former Secretary of State Henry Kissinger was famous for saying, "Power is the ultimate aphrodisiac." He also quipped, "The nice thing about being a celebrity is that when you bore people, they think it's their fault."
11. John 2:4.
12. "Do nothing out of selfish ambition or vain conceit. Rather, in humility value others above yourselves" (Philippians 2:3).
13. Rodney Stark, *The Rise of Christianity: How the Obscure, Marginal Jesus Movement Became the Dominant Religious Force in the Western World in a Few Centuries* (San Francisco: HarperSanFrancisco, 1996).
14. Paul Johnson, *Churchill* (New York: Penguin, 2009), 47.
15. Johnson, *Churchill*, 3.
16. Johnson, *Churchill*, 3.
17. Johnson, *Churchill*, 110.

18. 1 Corinthians 3:13.
19. Andy Crouch, *Culture Making: Recovering Our Creative Calling* (Downers Grove, IL: InterVarsity Press, 2008), 219.
20. See John 2:24–25.
21. See John 2:11, 22; 4:39, 53.
22. 1 Corinthians 11:1.

# Chapter 4: The Leader's Worldview

1. "Barna Survey Examines Changes in Worldview among Christians over the Past Thirteen Years," *Barna Group*, 6 March 2009, https://www.barna.org/barna-update/trans formation/252-barnasurvey-examines-changes-in-worldview -among-christians-over-the-past-13-years#.VpAocU2FOUk
2. John 18:36.
3. John 19:9–11 (emphasis added).
4. Philippians 2:6.
5. John 17:5.
6. John 17:2–3.
7. See Matthew 28:18–20; Acts 1:8.
8. John 17:4 (emphasis added).
9. Revelation 3:20 NLT.
10. John 17:6–8.
11. John 17:9–11.
12. See Matthew 16:22–23.
13. Eric Metaxas, *Bonhoeffer: Pastor, Martyr, Prophet, Spy* (Nashville: Nelson, 2010), 383.
14. Philippians 2:6.
15. See John 17:12–14, 19, 21.
16. John 17:23 NLT (emphasis added).
17. *The Book of Common Prayer* (New York: Oxford, 1979), 424.

# Chapter 5: The Humble Leader

1. Mark 10:42–45.
2. David Brooks, "High-Five Nation," *New York Times*, 5 September 2009, http://www.nytimes.com/2009/ 09/15/ opinion/15brooks.html
3. Brooks, "High-Five Nation."
4. Brooks, "High-Five Nation."
5. Michael Korda, *Ike: An American Hero* (New York: HarperCollins, 2007), 188.
6. William Manchester, *American Caesar: Douglas MacArthur 1880–1964* (Boston: Little, Brown, 1978), 3.
7. Korda, *Ike*, 45.
8. Dwight D. Eisenhower, "In Case of Failure," *Doing History Project*, http://doinghistoryproject.tripod.com/id17.html.
9. Matthew 11:28–30.
10. C. Peter Wagner, *Humility* (Ventura, CA: Gospel Light, 2002), 8.
11. 1 Peter 5:5.
12. C. S. Lewis, *Mere Christianity* (London: Macmillan, 1986), 92.
13. Eugene H. Peterson, *The Pastor: A Memoir* (New York: HarperOne, 2011), 157–58.
14. Luke 6:40.
15. Matthew 28:20 NLT.
16. 2 Timothy 4:7.
17. Lewis, *Mere Christianity*, 112.
18. Jeremiah 17:9–10.
19. Andrew Murray, *Humility: The Beauty of Holiness* (New York: Anson D. F. Randolph, n.d.), 133–34.

## Chapter 6: Becoming Something Else

1. James 3:1.
2. See 2 Timothy 2:2.
3. Matthew 18:2–6.
4. Some historians believe Jesus was not a carpenter but that his family was in business and that they were fairly wealthy by small-town standards. Otherwise, they wouldn't have been able to travel to Jerusalem for Passover. Jesus was called "Rabbi," which indicated some formal training. For more reading see Rodney Stark, *The Triumph of Christianity* (New York: HarperOne, 2011), 49–55.
5. *Truman*, PBS, 1997, http://www.pbs.org/wgbh/americanexperience/films/truman/.
6. David McCullough, *Truman* (New York: Simon & Schuster, 1993), 436.
7. Michael T. Benson, *Harry S. Truman and the Founding of Israel* (Westport, CT: Praeger, 1997), 64.
8. "Historical Notes: Giving Them More Hell," *Time*, December 3, 1973, 42.
9. This number is difficult to quantify in America because there are so many quasi clergy, ordained for tax advantages by Christian organizations and churches. This does not include the varied religious sects that defy categorization.
10. Paul put it this way in the context of spiritual gifts: "If God has given you leadership ability, take the responsibility seriously" (Romans 12:8 NLT).
11. See Matthew 13:44.

## Chapter 7: Leadership in Hard Times

1. John 12:23–26.
2. Peter DeVries, *The Blood of the Lamb* (Boston: Little, Brown, 1969).

3. DeVries, *The Blood of the Lamb*, 237–38.
4. See Job 42:1–6. In summary Job said, "Therefore I despise myself and repent in dust and ashes" (v. 6).
5. Kenneth Surin, *Theology and the Problem of Evil* (New York: Blackwell, 1986), 11.
6. Stanley Hauerwas, *Naming the Silences* (Grand Rapids: Eerdmans, 1990), 53.
7. *Führer* literally means "leader." The concept predates Hitler. It was the German concept of a superleader, a father figure for the fatherland.
8. Eric Metaxas, *Bonhoeffer: Pastor, Martyr, Prophet, Spy* (Nashville: Nelson, 2010), 139.
9. Metaxas, *Bonhoeffer*, 101.
10. Metaxas, *Bonhoeffer*, 99.
11. Metaxas, *Bonhoeffer*, 528.
12. Metaxas, *Bonhoeffer*, 532.
13. Dietrich Bonhoeffer, *Discipleship*, Dietrich Bonhoeffer Works 4 (Minneapolis: Augsburg Fortress, 2001), 43.
14. Eric Metaxas, "How Good Confronts Evil: Lessons from the Life and Death of Dietrich Bonhoeffer," in *Socrates in the City*, ed. Eric Metaxas (New York: Dutton, 2011), 342.
15. Dietrich Bonhoeffer, "Who Am I?," *Christianity and Crisis*, March 4, 1946.

## Chapter 8: The Rewards of Leadership

1. Ephesians 2:6.
2. John 10:10.
3. See Matthew 7:1–6.
4. See Matthew 15:1–14.
5. See Matthew 23:1–36; John 5:31–47.
6. Morris K. Udall, *Too Funny to Be President* (Tucson: University of Arizona Press, 2001).

7. 1 Thessalonians 2:19–20.
8. Eugene H. Peterson, *The Pastor: A Memoir* (San Francisco: HarperOne, 2011), 316.
9. 1 Timothy 4:15.
10. Bill Hull, *Christlike: The Pursuit of Uncomplicated Obedience* (Colorado Springs: NavPress, 2010).
11. *Choose the Life Journey* is a curriculum that includes *A Disciple's Guide* and five books with DVDs. The five-book set is entitled *Experience the Life*. It is connected to my book *Choose the Life: Exploring a Faith That Embraces Discipleship* (Colorado Springs: NavPress, 2004). It can be purchased through www.NavPress.com or www.Amazon.com/Bill Hull.
12. Dallas Willard, *Knowing Christ Today* (San Francisco: HarperOne, 2010), 210.
13. Eugene Peterson, *The Jesus Way: A Conversation on the Ways That Jesus Is the Way* (Grand Rapids: Eerdmans, 2007), 1.
14. Peterson, *The Jesus Way*, 2.
15. See 2 Corinthians 12:2–4.
16. 2 Timothy 4:6–8.
17. "Therefore anyone who sets aside one of the least of these commands and teaches others accordingly will be called least in the kingdom of heaven, but whoever practices and teaches these commands will be called great in the kingdom of heaven. For I tell you that unless your righteousness surpasses that of the Pharisees and the teachers of the law, you will certainly not enter the kingdom of heaven" (Matthew 5:19–20).
18. As cited in Malcolm Muggeridge, *A Third Testament* (New York: Little, Brown, 1976), 51.
19. See 1 Corinthians 3:10–15.

# Chapter 9: Leaders Are a Work in Progress

1. A. W. Tozer, *The Knowledge of the Holy* (New York: Harper & Row, 1961), 9.
2. C. S. Lewis, *The Weight of Glory: And Other Addresses* (New York: HarperCollins, 2001), 14.
3. Ephesians 2:10 NLT.
4. Hebrews 2:6–8 (quoting Psalm 8:4–6).
5. Philippians 2:14–16.
6. C. S. Lewis, *Mere Christianity* (New York: HarperCollins, 2001), 205.
7. Philippians 2:13.
8. As cited in Os Guinness, *The Call* (Waco, TX: Word, 1998), 4.
9. See 1 Timothy 3:1.
10. Philippians 2:13 (emphasis added).
11. See Colossians 3:5; Galatians 5:24; James 1:13–15; 2 Timothy 2:22.
12. 1 Kings 2:5–9.
13. C. S. Lewis, *The Weight of Glory*, 25–26.
14. Philippians 2:13.
15. Philippians 4:11–13.
16. May Sarton, "Now I Become Myself," in *Collected Poems (1930–1973)* (New York: Norton, 1974), 156, as quoted in Parker J. Palmer, *Let Your Life Speak* (San Francisco: Jossey-Bass, 2000), 9.
17. Palmer, *Let Your Life Speak*, 28–29.
18. Francis A. Schaeffer, *No Little People* (Downers Grove, IL: InterVarsity Press, 1974).
19. Luke 16:10 RSV.

# About the Author

**BILL HULL** has devoted his adult life to pastoring, teaching, and writing about Christ's command to make disciples. Bill's primary means for pursuing his mission as a discipleship evangelist has been pastoring for twenty years, teaching in more than fifty countries of the world, and authoring more than twenty books. Bill is now the leader of The Bonhoeffer Project, which is devoted to the creation of disciple-making leaders. You can learn more about Bill's work at TheBonhoefferProject.com and BillHull.net.

Twitter: @BillHull

Facebook: https://www.facebook.com/discipleship.billhull

# The Bonhoeffer Project

### Bill Hull

Bill is cofounder of The Bonhoeffer Project. Bill's passion is to help the church return to its disciple-making roots, and he considers himself a discipleship evangelist. This God-given desire has manifested itself in twenty years of pastoring and the authoring of many books. Two of his more important books, *Jesus Christ Disciplemaker*, and *The Disciple-Making Pastor*, have been in print twenty years.

### Brandon Cook

Brandon is cofounder of The Bonhoeffer Project and the lead pastor at Long Beach Christian Fellowship. He studied at Wheaton College (IL), Jerusalem University College, Brandeis University, and the Oxford Centre for Hebrew and Jewish Studies. He became convinced that his work — and the work of the church — is to become fully committed to discipleship and making disciple makers.

## Goal

The goal of The Bonhoeffer Project is to encourage each participant to become a disciple-making leader. Once that decision has been made, then the goal is to provide the participant with the knowledge necessary to carry out a plan for making disciples who also will make disciples. The Bonhoeffer Project firmly believes that this is best done in a community of like-minded persons. That is why the project itself is a community.

## Plan

Making disciples requires intentionality. William Law in his book *A Serious Call to a Devout and Holy Life*, made this point: the reason people don't change behavior is that they never really intend to do so. The intention to make disciples requires a plan, and if you have no plan, you don't really intend to do it. The Bonhoeffer Project helps each participant craft a plan that is biblically sound and a good fit for their ministry context. Each of the ten gatherings will focus on a specific subject that is followed by a monthly project.

## Contact

www.thebonhoefferproject.com

# Conversion & Discipleship

## You Can't Have One without the Other

*Bill Hull*

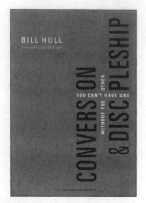

Discipleship occurs when someone answers the call to learn from Jesus how to live his or her life—as though Jesus were living it. The end result is that the disciple becomes the kind of person who naturally does what Jesus did.

How the church understands salvation and the gospel is the key to recovering a biblical theology of discipleship. Our doctrines of grace and salvation, in some cases, actually prevent us from creating an expectation that we are to be disciples of Jesus. A person can profess to be a Christian and yet still live under the impression that they don't need to actually follow Jesus. Being a follower is seen as an optional add-on, not a requirement. It is a choice, not a demand. Being a Christian today has no connection with the biblical idea that we are formed into the image of Christ.

In this ground-breaking new book, pastor and author Bill Hull shows why our existing models of evangelism and discipleship fail to actually produce followers of Jesus. He looks at the importance of recovering a robust view of the gospel and taking seriously the connection between conversion—answering the call to follow Jesus—and discipleship—living like the one we claim to follow.

*Available in stores and online!*